Peanuts™ Gang
Collectibles

An Unauthorized Handbook and Price Guide

Jan Lindenberger
with Cher Porges

Schiffer
Publishing Ltd ®

4880 Lower Valley Road, Atglen, PA 19310 USA

Copyright © 1998 by Jan Lindenberger
Library of Congress Catalog Card Number: 98-85649

Designed by Bonnie M. Hensley
Layout by Randy L. Hensley
Typeset in Comic MS Sans/Times New Roman

ISBN: 0-7643-0671-5
Printed in China
1 2 3 4

Published by Schiffer Publishing Ltd.
4880 Lower Valley Road
Atglen, PA 19310
Phone: (610) 593-1777; Fax: (610) 593-2002
E-mail: Schifferbk@aol.com

In Europe, Schiffer Books are distributed by
Bushwood Books
6 Marksbury Avenue Kew Gardens
Surrey TW9 4JF England
Phone: 44 (0) 181 392-8585; Fax: 44 (0) 181 392-9876
E-Mail: Bushwd@aol.com

Please write for a free catalog.
This book may be purchased from the publisher.
Please include $3.95 for shipping.
Please try your bookstore first.
We are interested in hearing from authors
with book ideas on related subjects.

Contents

Acknowledgments

I wish to give a very special thank you to Cher Porges and her family. Without Cher this guide to Peanuts Collectibles would not have been possible. We worked many weeks and long hard hours to give this project the value it deserves. Her patience in arranging and rearranging her vast collection was greatly appreciated. Along the way she had found things she had forgotten were there. The information for this Peanuts price guide came from her years of knowledge and research.

Between the diet sodas and mustard pretzels, and the privilege of me sleeping near the prized "Peanuts and Snoopy Room", this Peanuts price guide was born. With the large collection it turned out to be, we felt it warranted two editions of the Peanuts Gang books. Also because we had recently published two editions of price guides on Snoopy! This meant longer hours, more days, and more diet soda. But the end result wound up being four much needed, all color, information and price guides. Mrs. Porges didn't mind the extra work as this gives every collector of Snoopy and The Peanuts Gang an up-to-date information and price guide.

Again thanks Cher, it was wonderful working with you and I have gained you and your family as my valued friends. That's the best part of this job

Thanks also to; Laurel Sherry from New Holstein, Wisconsin. Laurel is the show promoter for the Mid West Snoopy Swap Meet. Her patience in allowing me to photograph on show day was greatly appreciated, as was her encouragement to do these 4 books. Thanks too to all the dealers at the show who let me photograph their Snoopy and Peanut gang collectibles. For information about the Snoopy Swap Meet contact Laurel by phone or fax, at 920-898-5578 or by E-Mail at Cowtown@fdldotnet.com.

Also thanks to Warren and Joyce Chamberlin, Mishawauka, Indiana and Rose Elkins, Saint Louis, Missouri, and Joel Marton from Colorado Springs, Colorado, for opening up their homes to photograph their collections and giving us added information for the Peanuts Gang information and price guides.

Consetta, Cher, Andrew and Woody Too

Introduction

Where can you find dogs, birds, a round headed kid, a kid with a security blanket, a loudmouthed girl in a booth, a musician, an African-American, humor, and wit, all with psychological and theological undertones? For nearly 50 years all this and more have been the winning ingredients of Peanuts.

Charlie Brown, Patty, Shermy and Snoopy came from humble beginnings, in 7 newspapers. The gang got off to a slow start with subscribers coming and going. Only 18-20 newspapers subscribed during the first year. After some promotional planning, with small ads introducing the Peanuts gang on an individual basis, growth finally occurred during the second year. At last, in 1952 it was time for the Sunday feature.

Also in 1952, John Selby, editor-in-chief at Rhinehart & Company and a personal fan of Peanuts, decided that his favorite comic strip deserved a book. With the publication of *Peanuts* the book in 1952, the comic book reprint business was off to a great start. With the exception of 1953, there has been a minimum of one book of reprinted Peanuts strips published per year. Not a bad record for this delightful comic!

What started out as a small group of four, Charlie Brown, Snoopy, and the all-but-forgotten Patty and Shermy, grew slowly into the cast of characters we now know and love. 1951 saw the introduction of Violet and Schroeder, who was soon playing Beethoven on a toy piano. Lucy and Linus Van Pelt arrived in 1952. Pig Pen began kicking up dirt in 1954. Sally Brown, Charlie Brown's sister, crawled into the strip in 1959. Patricia Reichardt, better known as Peppermint Patty slid into home for the first time in 1966. Her best friend Marcie joined her in 1971. Birds resembling Woodstock have been flitting around since the late 1960s. In 1970 Woodstock was officially named after the famous concert. Franklin, our African-American friend, came in 1968. The Van Pelt household had a new arrival in 1973, named Rerun. The Beagle Scouts, Woodstock's feathered colleagues, marched into the strip in the mid-1970s, and were given individual names, such as Conrad, Oliver, and Bill in the late 1970s. Snoopy's first sibling from the Daisy Hill Puppy Farm, his brother Spike, was introduced in 1975. Next, his sister, Belle, arrived in 1976. She was followed by her brother, Marbles, in 1982. Then came brother Olaf in 1989, and another brother named Andy in 1994. Of course this is not a complete list, but with all the characters coming and going, its impossible to list them all.

The character of Snoopy has changed immensely over the years. You can tell this by his five different two-dimensional copyright dates. When Snoopy first appeared in 1950 he always walked on four feet or sat on his haunches. This was his earliest copyright date. He earned another copyright in 1956 when he was shown dancing on two feet with his head flying high. He was walking on two feet all the time by 1958, thus earning his third copyright date. His fourth copyright came in 1965, with his ears tucked under his aviators hat and goggles covering his eyes, as the Flying Ace he began his battles against the Red Baron. His final copyright date came in 1971, when Joe Cool appeared on the scene. Through all these changes he still kept his lovable personality.

Note: The copyright dates on the item does not reflect the year of manufacturing, only the year when the character on the piece was originally created. Thus, a piece with a 1965 copyright date may have been manufactured from 1965 through today!

The creator of our favorite gang is Charles Monroe Schulz. Charles Schulz's uncle gave him the nickname Sparky at the tender age of 2 days in 1922, after "Spark Plug," a horse featured in Barney Google comics. This would prove prophetic. As Schulz was growing up in St. Paul, Minnesota, he would savor all the comics he could obtain, dreaming that his own artwork would be published someday.

After learning his craft through a mail order art school, he began his career as a teacher for that same school. He then went to New York in 1950 to seek publication of his comic strip "Lil Folks" with United Features Syndicate. While the Syndicate liked Schulz's characters, they did not care for the name and soon changed it to "Peanuts," a decision of which Schulz was not fond. Some editors of the Syndicate wanted to downplay the roll of Snoopy in the strip. Luckily Schulz gave Snoopy the prominent place he deserves in his work.

Over the years, countless items have been manufactured celebrating the Peanuts Gang. Even though this book can only scratch the surface of what is available, we hope it will give you a sampling of the vast range of wonderful collectibles that are available.

Hints for Collectors

By far the best place to buy Snoopy Collectibles is the Mid West Snoopy Swap Meet. This show and sale is organized by Laurel Sherry. One may contact Laurel at 1723 Monroe St. New Holstein, Wisconsin. 53061 for information on the next meet. Phone/fax: 920-898- 5578. E-mail: cowtown@fdldotnet.com.

Several hundred people who love Snoopy get together to buy, sell, trade and talk Snoopy. You will find Snoopy and the Peanuts Gang in abundance. The prices are more than fair and the spirit among the sellers is very cheerful. To the collector, it's better than Christmas. You can tell they all love that beagle!

Searching for Snoopy is fun and challenging. While waiting for the Snoopy Swap Meet, a good way to start a collection is to scour garage sales and flea markets. The prices are usually negotiable but the merchandise isn't always mint. The more flaws the less you should have to pay.

Antique Malls can also be fruitful. Prices vary extremely but, depending on condition and how knowledgeable the seller is, merchandise can be reasonably had. If the item catches your eye and you must have it, it's quite convenient to purchase it at the mall or antique shop. Remember the old slogan, "You snooze, you loose?" Purchase it when you see it or it may not be there when you go back.

If you have a bit more cash, toy shows are wonderful. Prices can be negotiated slightly and merchandise is generally in good condition. There are also several toy magazines which have advertisements from all over the country. This is a good way to track down hard-to-find treasures.

For new items a good source, especially around the holiday season when special things come on the market, is Knotts Berry Farms, Camp Snoopy.

Whatever path you choose to take in your search for Snoopy, remember the real search is for fun!

I hope you enjoy this Snoopy collectibles guide. Prices may vary according to area, availability, and condition. Please take this book with you on your "Snoopy search" and happy hunting!

Metal mini tin from Sanrio, Japan. Determined. 1990s. 2.2" x 4". $8-12.

Cookin' with the Gang

Ceramic "'Snoopy' Brown Bag Pet Goodies" jar. Con Agra. Early 1980s. $200-250.

Ceramic Snoopy cookie jar. Unknown maker. Older. Very rare. $300-350.

Ceramic items. Heart box, "Love" on lid. 2-1/2". 1977. $35-45. Egg cup, (Determined) Snoopy dressed as chef. 4-1/2". 1979. $65-75. Cookie jar or candy jar. 7-1/2". 1979. $125-150. Jam jar with plastic spoon. 4-1/4" 1977. $75-90. Mustard jar. 3". 1977. $75-90. Salt and pepper. 4-1/2" Snoopy-3-1/2" Woodstock on shaker. Mid 1970s. $60-75 set.

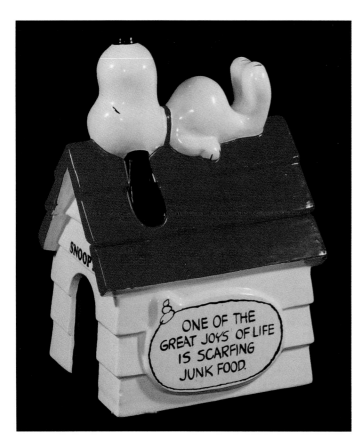 

Ceramic Snoopy on doghouse cookie jar. Front and back view. 8" x 11-1/2" x 6". Con Agra. Early 1980s. $300-350.

Ceramic Snoopy cookie jar. 11". Determined. McCoy. Early 1970s. $225-275. Also came unpainted,-all white except for Snoopy letters painted black. $100-150.

Ceramic Snoopy cookie jar. Very rare. Marked "Copyright 1958-1966 United Syndicate Features." (according to E. Supnick's book this one is unmarked) 10-1/2" x 7". $500- 600.

Ceramic Snoopy chef cookie jar. 11". Determined.
1977. $225-275. 8", $150-200.

Ceramic Woodstock cookie jar. Benjamin and Medwin. Early 1990s.
$35-45.

Ceramic Charlie Brown cookie jar. Benjamin and Medwin. Early 1990s.
$35-45.

Ceramic Lucy cookie jar. Benjamin
and Medwin. Early 1990s. $35-45.

Ceramic Charlie Brown and Lucy salt and pepper set. Benjamin and Medwin. Early 1990s. $12-18 set with box.

Ceramic Peanuts Gang magnets. Benjamin and Medwin. Mid 1990s. $2-3 each.

Ceramic Flying Ace cookie jar. Mid 1990s. Benjamin & Medwin. $40-50.

Ceramic sugar, creamer, salt and pepper set. Willitts. Sold individually. 1990. Sugar and creamer $30-40 each. Salt and pepper on couch. $40-50. All came in boxes.

Snoopy and the Peanut Gang Dish Set. Ironstone. Taylor Smith & Taylor. 1978. $45-55.

3-piece Peanuts Gang, ceramic dish set from Determined productions, Johnson Brothers. Mid 1970s. $50-75 with box. Bowl not shown in set.

Ceramic teapot and cups. 4-3/4" x 6-1/2" teapot. 2-1/2" x 1-3/4". Japan. $75-100 set.

Ceramic soda cup. Determined. 1970s. $25-35.

Ceramic Peanuts Gang Chili bowl. Mid 1970s. Determined. $15-20.

Ceramic cup. "Beagles Are My Favorite People." Determined. 1980s. $10-15.

Ceramic Woodstock and Flying Ace cups. Applause. Early 1990s. $20-25 each with box.

Ceramic coffee cups. Applause and, probably, Willitts. 1990s. $10-15.

3 ceramic coffee cups. Determined. 1980s. $10-15 each.

Ceramic "Mall of America," Peanuts Gang coffee mugs. Camp Snoopy, Bloomington, Minnesota. Mid 1990s. $6-10.

Ceramic cups. Willitts. Late 1980s. $10-15 each.

Front and side views of ceramic Lucy and Snoopy cup. 1990s. Determined. $8-12.

Ceramic Christmas coffee cup, 1976. Determined. $12-18.

Ceramic mug. Snoopy laying on doghouse. Raised design. Determined. Mid 1970s. $25-35.

Ceramic mug. Snoopy as Joe Cool standing in front of yellow star. Determined. Unknown date. $25-35.

Ceramic mugs. Front and back views. Determined. Mid 1970s. Snoopy as Forlorn Flying Ace. "Girls and root beer are not the answer" on the back. 5" $40- 50. Snoopy & Woodstock. "Actually, we Joe Cools are scared to death of chicks" on back. 5". $40-50. Snoopy with Woodstock next to him with different sports outfits. 4-1/4". $20-30.

Ceramic steins. Determined. 1970s. Snoopy as Joe Cool. $30-40. Snoopy on handle. $25-35. Snoopy as Joe Cool with Woodstock. $35-45.

Peanuts Gang, drinking glasses. McDonalds premiums. 1983. $4-6 each.

Plastic cups from McDonald's. Special promotions from 1983s. $18-25 set.

Manager's Snoopy promotional glass from McDonalds, front and back view, 1983. Very rare.

Plastic Lucy Oscar Mayer cup. 1990s. $3-4.

15

Juice jug and glasses. "Snoopy's Kitchen." Anchor Hocking. Late 1970s. $20-25 with box.

Glass Snoopy root beer mug. Anchor Hocking. late 1970s early 80s. $10-15.

Juice set, pitcher and glasses. Peanuts gang. Anchor Hocking. Late 1970s. $20-30 in box.

Set of Peanuts Gang glasses in plastic carrier. Anchor Hocking. Late 1970s early 1980s. $15-20 set.

Glass vases. Anchor Hocking. Late 1970s. $10-15.

Glass vase from Anchor Hocking. Late 1970s. $10-15.

Large vase, Snoopy giving Woodstock flowers. Anchor Hocking. Late 1970s. $10-15.

Peanuts Gang glass vases. Anchor Hocking. Late 1970s. $10-12.

WW1 Flying Ace Float Making Kit. Came with A & W glasses and utensils. 1990s. Rare. $60-75.

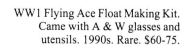

Ceramic nut dishes. Left to right. 2-1/2" x 3". 1978. 4" x 7-1/2". 1977. 2-1/2" x 3". 1979. $90-125 each.

3 piece child's set. Peanuts Gang. Pecoware. Late 1980s early 90s. $20-25 with box.

Vinyl ice bucket. Snoopy and Woodstock in top hats. Shelton Ware. 10" x 7-3/4". 1979. $100-125.

Melamine Shelina plate. 1980s. $12-15.

Peanuts Gang plastic divided dish. Pecoware. 1990s. $8-12.

Snoopy plastic child's dish set. Pecoware. Late 1980s-90s. $20-30.

Melamine divided dish set. Pecoware. 1990s. $5-7 each.

Plastic Peanuts Gang dish with suction cups. Pecoware. 1990s. $10-15.

Aluminum Charlie Brown cake pan with plastic head for the cake. Wilton. 1980s $20-25.

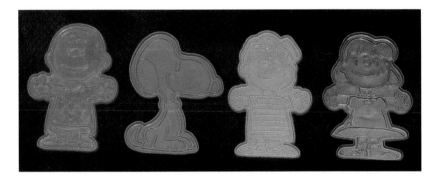

Plastic Peanut gang cookie cutters. Hallmark. Early 1970s. Cookie cutter prices reflect in package mint. $75-100 set.

Aluminum Flying Ace, cake pan. Wilton. Late 1980s. $20-25.

Plastic heart-shaped cookie cutters. Hallmark. Mid 1970s. $75-150.

Plastic set of Peanuts Gang cookie cutters. Hallmark. Mid 1970s. $75-100 set.

Lets Do Lunch and Party

Vinyl lunch boxes. Vinyl is more difficult
to find and the most desirable. King
Seeley. Mid 1970s. $50-65.

Metal Peanuts King Seeley lunch box with
King Seeley thermos. 1980s. $20-30.

Vinyl lunch boxes. King Seeley. Mid 1970s. $50-65.

Metal Peanuts Gang lunch box from Thermos. 1978. $18-30.

Plastic Peanuts Gang lunch box from Thermos. 1990s. $10-15.

Plastic Peanuts Gang lunch boxes with King Seeley thermos. 1990s. $10-15.

Fabric kid's lunch tote. Mid 1990s. Aladdin. $8-12.

Peanuts Gang thermos set. King Seeley thermos. 1969. $5-7 each.

Birthday paper cups, plates, napkins of the Daisy Hill Puppies. Mid 1990s. $3-5 each.

Peanuts Gang , paper party plates. Hallmark. Late 1970s. $4-7.

Paper party table cover. Came in cello wrap. Hallmark. Late 1970s. $4-7.

Plastic bottle Caps. 1980s. Wecolite Co.. $5-7 each in package.

Plastic plates with the Flying Ace. Hallmark. Early 1970s. $10-15 in package.

Ceramic Peanuts Gang trivet. Mid 1990s. Mall of America, Mn. $6-10.

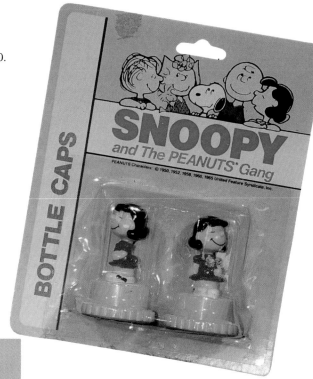

Plastic Lucy bottle caps. Wecolite Co. 1980s. $5-7 in package.

Peanuts vinyl placemat. 1990s. $3-5.

Plastic placemat. Sally, Charlie Brown, Snoopy. 1990s. $8-12.

Plastic placemat with Linus and Snoopy sucking their thumbs. Greenbrier Studios. 1980s. $4-6.

Plastic placemat. Snoopy and Charlie Brown. Greenbrier Studios. 1980s. $4-6.

Paper cups from Dixie. 100-5 oz. 1980s. $7-10.

The Peanuts Gang cup dispenser. Dixie. Early 1980s. $15-20 with box.

Dixie paper cups. 1980s. $7-9 each.

Canvas party apron from Chex cereal.
Peanuts Gang. Early 1990s. Adult
sizes $20-25. Child sizes $15-20.

Terrycloth apron. 1980s. Tastemaker by
Stevens. Came as set with potholder.
$15-20 mint apron. $20-25 mint set.

Peanuts Gang birthday cake decorating set.
Hallmark. 1970s. $10-15.

Ralston Rice Chex cereal. Late 1980s-90s. $3-5 each.

Chex cereal boxes. 1980-90s. $3-4 each.

Packets of seasonings to make Chex party mix. Originally came free in box of Chex cereal. 1990s. $2-3 each.

Jelly jars from Smuckers with the Peanuts gang. Different characters molded in glasses. Different fruit spread for each character. Mid 1990s. $6-10 empty. $8-12 full.

Peanut Butter plastic jars from Smuckers with the Peanuts Gang. Creamy and crunchy. Mid 1990s. $6-10 empty. $12-15 full.

Metal popcorn snack tins. Confections-Chicago. 1990s. $7-10 each.

Holiday Heath Milk Chocolate bars with Charlie Brown & Friends Chocolate Bar. Mid 1990s. $2-5.

Glass Charlie Brown peanut jars. Probably 1980s. 7-1/2". Georgia Food and Nut Processors. $8-10 each.

Metal store display. Dolly Madison snacks. 3 shelves. 24" x 18" x 17". Late 1970s. $100-150.

Fancy Plates

Ceramic plate. Mothers Day 1975. Schmid. $25-35 in box.

Valentines Day ceramic plate. Schmid. 1981. $40- 60 with box.

Ceramic Mother's Day plate. Schmid. 1972. $35-50 with box.

Ceramic Mother's Day plate. Schmid. 1976. $25-35 with box.

Ceramic Christmas plate. 1973. Schmid. Most valued plate. $250-300 with box.

Ceramic Christmas plate. Schmid. 1974. $60-80 with box.

Ceramic Christmas plate. Schmid. 1975. $25-35 with box.

Ceramic Snoopy Christmas plate. 1990. Willitts. $30-40 with box.

Ceramic Christmas plate. 1991. Willitts. Very few made. Hard to find. $100-125 with box.

Ceramic Christmas plate. Determined Production for Joy's Inc. 1980s-1990s. $25-35.

Fine porcelain, Limited Edition. Franklin Mint Heirloom Collection. Merry Christmas, Charlie Brown plate. Early 1990s. $40-50.

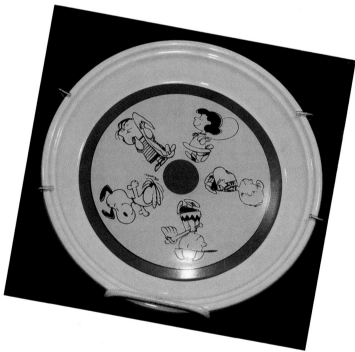

China plate. This is the plate for a 3 piece place setting which also includes cup and bowl. Iroquois. For Determined. Early 1970s. Complete set with box. $75-100. Plate alone. $20-30.

Ceramic 30th Anniversary plate. 1950-1980. Oversized. Schmid. $50-60 with box.

Charlie Brown ceramic plate. Danbury Mint. Limited edition. Early 1990s. $50-60.

Snoopy Senior Hockey Tournament ceramic plate. 1995. World Wide Line. $40-50.

Ceramic mini plates. Schmid Athletic set. Complete set shown but were sold individually. 1983. $50-60 each, $250-275 set, with boxes.

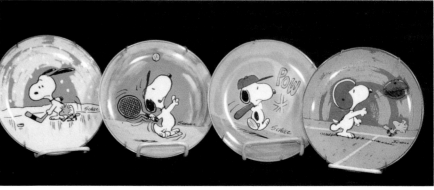

Let's Figure This

These Figures Stand Alone

Ceramic Peanuts Gang figurines. These unlicenced figures are fashioned after the Hungerfords. The molds were probably made in the 1960s. Since these were hand-painted, each one is a little different. The finish is painted on and not refired, thus the matte finish. $10-15 each.

Rubber Peanuts Gang toys (compare to ceramic figures). Hungerford Toys. These toys originally came in a cello bag with cartoon panel top. An extremely rare find in package! Came in two sizes except for Pig Pen, Sally and Schroeder. Snoopy, being the most popular, is also the most common. Schroeder with piano is the rarest. 1958. Collectors would pay $100-150 just for the piano. Snoopy 5". Charlie Brown, Lucy, Linus. 7"- 7-3/4". $80-150 each. Snoopy 7". Sally 7". Schroeder 7". $30-90 each. Lucy, Linus, Charlie Brown, Snoopy. $30-90. Pig Pen, Sally. $75- 125. Schroeder with piano. $200-300.

These Figures Stand, Wobble, & Nod

Peanuts Gang papier mache nodders. Lego. These highly prized nodders are a collector's must have. Because of their age it is difficult to find a set with everyone just perfect. Fact is, one will probably be purchasing them individually, when one can find them. Of course Snoopy was the most popular, so he is easier to find and more reasonably priced. Pigpen and Schroeder are rarer and a little more. 1959. Snoopy, Charlie Brown, Lucy, Linus. $50-75. Pigpen, Schroeder $60-85.

Peanuts Gang nodders. Papier mache. Lego. 1958. $50-75 each. $350-500 set.

Articulated Snoopy, ceramic. His arms and legs move. Determined. Early 1980s. $350-450.

Papier mache bobble head Charlie Brown by Determined Prod. 1976. $25-35.

Glass figurines. Marcolin Art Crystal. Made in Sweden. Snoopy laying on stomach. 7-1/4" x 2-1/2". Snoopy sitting 4-3/4" x 3-1/4". 1990s. $100-125 each.

Papier mache bobble head Woodstock by Determined Prod. 1976. $20-30.

Peanut gang nodder set. Ceramic. Japan. Late 1980s/1990s.
Made by Jump for Joy. $30-40 each. $200- 250 set.

Snoopy figure scene. Papier mache.
Determined. Early 1970s. $30-40.

Lucy and Linus figure scenes. Determined. Early 1970s. $20-40.

Figure scenes. Determined. Papier mache. Early 1970s. $30-40 each.

Snoopy figure scene. Papier mache. Determined.
Early 1970s. $30-40.

Snoopy and Woodstock figure scenes. Papier mache. Determined. Early 1970s. $30-40 each.

Charlie Brown and Snoopy papier mache figure scenes. Determined. Early 1970s. $20-30.

Figure scenes. Determined. Papier mache. 1970s. $40-50 each.

Figure Scene. Determined. Papier mache. Baseball team. Early 1970s. $150-175.

Linus and Sally papier mache figure scene. Determined. Early 1970s. $20-30.

Peanuts Gang baseball ceramic banks from Japan. Made by Jump for Joy, late 1980s - early 1990s. $30-40 each, $200-250 set.

Lucy, Charlie Brown, Sally, Snoopy, Schroeder, Linus ceramic banks. 8.5"-9". Hand-painted in Italy. 1969. $150-200 each.

Ceramic Peanut Gang, banks. 6". Hand painted in Italy. Determined. 1969. $100-125 each.

Charlie Brown, Lucy, Snoopy, Linus
hand-painted ceramic banks. 6". Italy.
1969. $75-100 each.

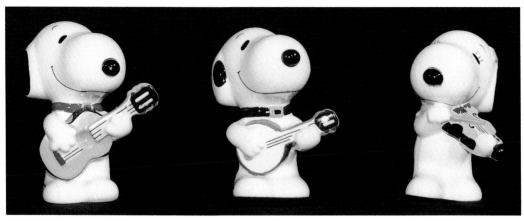

Ceramic banks. Set of 6. Snoopy and
Snoopy's brothers and sisters.
Snoopy, Marbles, Belle, Olof, Spike,
Andy. 4.5". Made in Japan. Mid
1990s. $300-400 set.

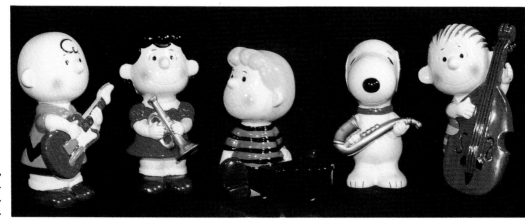

Ceramic banks. Charlie Brown,
Lucy, Schroeder, Snoopy, Linus.
Made in Japan. Mid 1990s.
$300-400 set.

Ceramic Snoopy inside money pot. 5-1/2" x 3-1/2". Denz. Japan. Mid 1990s. $60-70.

Ceramic Snoopy wearing scarf bank. 6-1/2" x 5-1/2". Denz. Japan. Mid 1990s. $60-75.

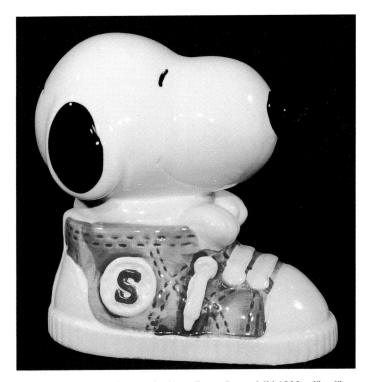

Ceramic Snoopy inside tennis shoes. Denz. Japan. Mid 1990s. 6" x 6". $60-70.

Ceramic Snoopy sitting with flowers, bank. Denz. Japan. Mid 1990s. 6" x 4-1/2". $60-70.

Ceramic Snoopy with instruments, banks. Denz. Japan. Mid 1990s. 5" x 4". $60-70 each.

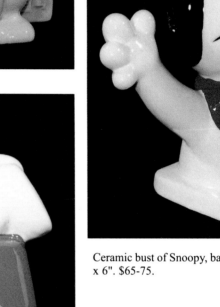

Ceramic bust of Snoopy, bank. Denz. Japan. Mid 1990s. 5" x 6". $65-75.

Ceramic Snoopy bank. 7-1/2" x 5". Denz. Japan. Mid 1990s. $60-70.

Papier mache ice cream cone bank. 4-1/2". Made in England. Mid 1990s. $35-40.

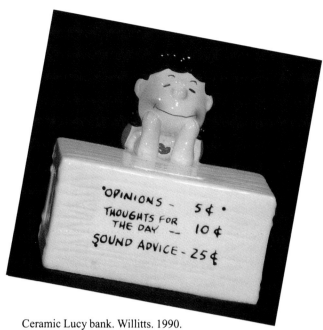

Ceramic Lucy bank. Willitts. 1990. $20-25.

Ceramic Snoopy bank. 11". Made in Japan. $100-125.

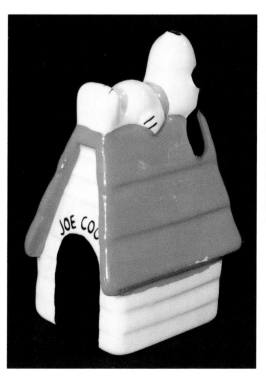

Ceramic Snoopy as Joe Cool, bank (Front and back). 2" x 3-1/4" x 1-1/2". Willitts. 1990. $20-30.

Ceramic Snoopy and Woodstock bank. Willitts. 1990. (Sticker on top states "40 years of happiness"). 7-1/2". $40-50.

Ceramic train bank. Willitts. 7-1/2" x 8" x 3-1/2". 1990. $45-55.

Ceramic Snoopy-shaped bank. Unknown maker and year. 5-1/2" x 4-1/2". $30-45.

Patriotic Snoopy bank. 10-1/2" tall. 40th anniversary. Willitts. 1990s. $75-100.

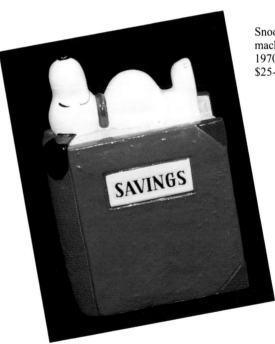

Snoopy savings bank. Papier mache. Determined. Mid 1970s. Also available in gold. $25-40.

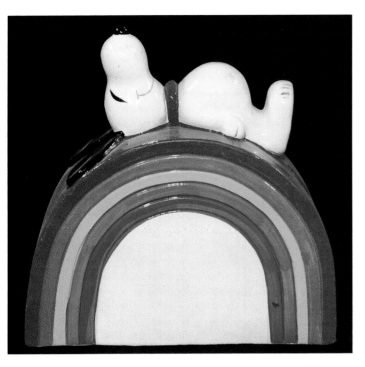

Papier mache Snoopy laying on rainbow, bank. Determined. 1976. $25-35.

Papier mache, Snoopy laying on penny, bank. Determined. Early 1980s. $35-45.

Papier mache, Belle wearing pink dress, bank. Determined. 1981. $30-40.

Papier mache Snoopy bank. 5-1/2". Determined. Mid 1970s. $30-40.

Papier mache banks. Animal series. Determined. Mid 1970s. 4-1/2". $40-60 each.

Papier mache Snoopy in sun glasses bank.
Determined. Early 1980s. 5-1/2". $30-40.

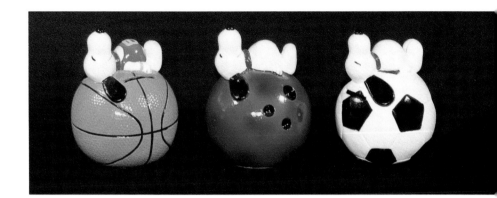

Papier mache banks. Sport series. Determined. 1970s. 4". $40-70 each.

Papier mache Snoopy fireman
bank. Ideal. 1977. 5-1/2". $40-50.

Papier mache banks. Transportation series. Determined. 1977. 5" to 5-1/2". $30-40 each.

Papier mache Joe Cool bank. Ideal. 1977. 6". $40-50.

Ceramic banks. Hat series. Snoopy in different outfits. 5". Determined. 1979. $30-45 each.

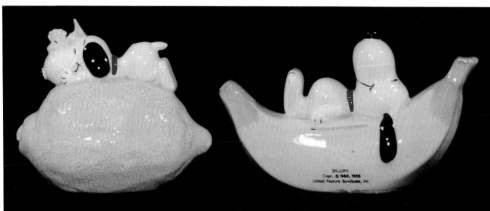

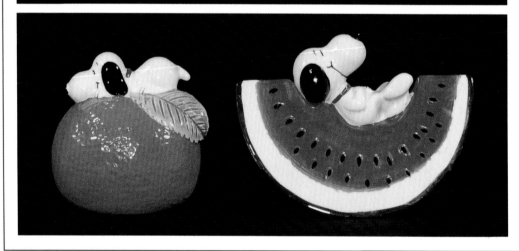

Ceramic Fruit series banks. Determined. 1976. $40-60 each. Also made in papier mache.

Ceramic square banks. Baby blocks. 3-1/4". Determined. Mid 1970s. $45-50 each.

Ceramic standing Woodstock bank. Determined. Mid 1970s. 6". $35-45.

Ceramic Junk Food series banks. Determined. 1979 3-1/2" x 4-1/2". French fries & chocolate ice cream cone. 3-1/2" x 4 x-1/2" hamburger. 4" x 6" hot dog. $45-55 each.

Ceramic Snoopy-holding-Woodstock bank. Determined. 6-1/4". $60-75.

Ceramic sitting Snoopy bank. Determined. Mid 1970s. 16". $350-400.

Ceramic sitting Snoopy banks. 5-1/2" and 5". Determined. Mid 1970s. $25-35 each.

Ceramic Snoopy bank. Ideal or could be a later version by Determined. 3-1/2" x 5-1/4" x 3". 1977. $50-60.

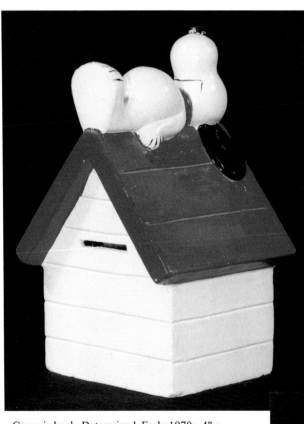

Ceramic bank. Determined. Early 1970s. 4" x 6-3/4". $25-35.

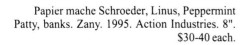

Papier mache Schroeder, Linus, Peppermint Patty, banks. Zany. 1995. Action Industries. 8". $30-40 each.

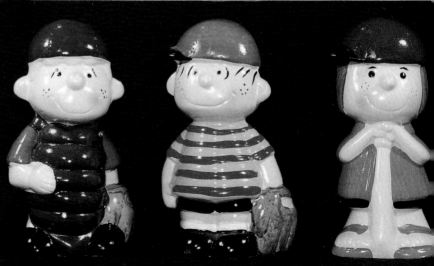

Hard plastic banks. Snoopy playing tennis. Snoopy playing golf. Snoopy in red diaper with yellow pin. 1980s. Danara. $20-30 each.

Hard plastic banks. Snoopy with skis. Snoopy in green pajamas. Snoopy as graduate. 1980s. $20-30 each.

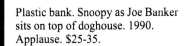

Plastic bank. Snoopy as Joe Banker sits on top of doghouse. 1990. Applause. $25-35.

Clear plastic cylindrical shape, "Premium dog food bank." 1970s. $30-40.

Plastic Woodstock on egg in nest bank. 1990. Applause. $20-30.

Tin bank. globe-shaped, Snoopy as athlete in different sports. 1980s. Ohio Art. $30-40.

Tin barrel-shaped bank. Snoopy and Woodstock with clock on side. 1990s. Determined. $15-25.

Heavy cardboard "Save the World" Snoopy and the gang bank with arms outstretched. Made in England. 1990s. $10-15.

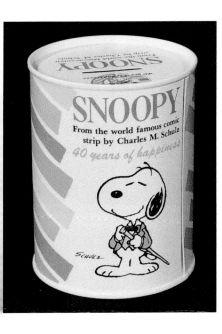

Tin Snoopy with cane bank. "40 years of happiness/" Determined. Japan, 1990s. $20-30.

Lunch box style tin bank. 1990s. Denz. $20-30.

Wonderful Sets

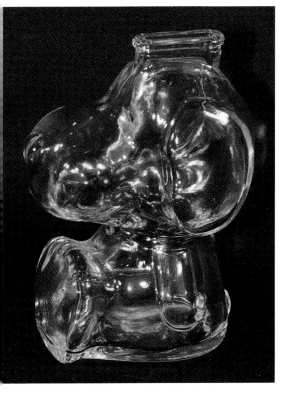

Glass Anchor Hocking sitting Snoopy bank. "United Features Syndicate" must be etched on bottom. Later issues had paper stickers. 1979. $50-60 original. $5-8 for paper label.

Christmas Pageant from Willitts. Bisque figures and cardboard creche. Issued 2 years. 1st year musical creche. 2nd year added Schroeder. $125-150 complete. Figures were sold separately, but creche was sold only with the set of figures. Musical Creche sold separately. The cardboard creche is very rare. 1989-1990.

Porcelain Peanuts Gang figurines on wooden baseball diamond. Willitts. 1990. $200-250 set.

Porcelain figures with wooden musical creche. Willitts. Early 1990s. Figures 1.5". Musical creche. 7-3/4" x 10" x 5". $150-200 set.

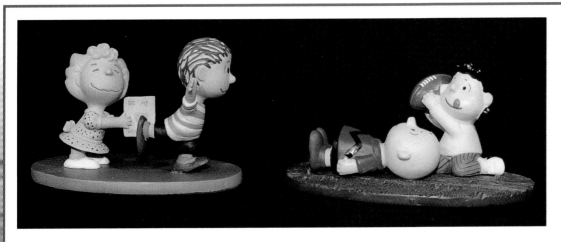

Figurines. Danbury Mint. Resin. Sold individually each being numbered and came with a certificate. 1990s. Danbury Mint offered a special: if all twelve figures were purchased, they would furnish a decorative wood shelf for display. $35-50 each. 12 figures with shelf $450-500 complete.

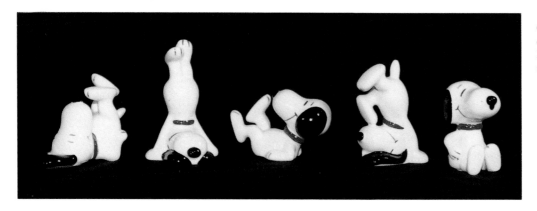

Ceramic figurines. Snoopy in five different poses. Tallest is 2.5". Determined. Early 1980s. $125-150 set.

Plastic Kinder figures from Europe. Came in chocolate candy (egg-shaped). 1-3/4". Take figures apart and put them together. Most 3 or 4 pieces. Recent. Mid 1990s. $8-10 each.

Resin cake toppers. Flambro. 1997. $20-25 each.

Resin figurines. Flambro. 1997.
3" to 4". $20-25 each.

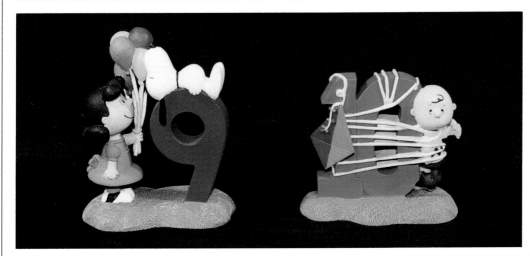

Light My Fire

Paper mache Peanuts Gang candle
holders. Hallmark. Early 1970s.
$15-25 each.

Wax candle. Hallmark. Mid to late 1970s. $20-25.

Candle Snoopy. Hallmark. Late 1970s. $17-25.

Wax candles. Snoopy and Charlie Brown. Hallmark. Mid to late 1970s. $15-20 each.

Ceramic votive candle. Hallmark. $20-25.

Small glass votive candle. Hallmark. Early 1970s. Baseball scene with Woodstock, Linus, Lucy, Schroeder, Charlie Brown, Peppermint Patty, Snoopy and Thibault and Five. The last two character's presence is what gives this piece its value. $50-75.

56

Daisy Hill Puppies candles from
Hallmark. 1990s. $3-4.

Ceramic Peanuts Gang
cup. Mid 1990s. Mall of
America, MN. $6-10.

Itty Bitty Statues

Ceramic statues. 1-1/2". Aviva.
Late 1970s. $15-20 each.

And the Trophy Goes To...

Plastic scenic trophy Snoopy dancing for Woodstock. Early 1970s. $20-30.

Linus trophy. Aviva. 1970s/80s. $10-15.

Plastic trophy. Aviva. Early 1970s through the mid 1980s. Snoopy being the most popular. The character trophies were more difficult to find thus they are more valuable. $10-15 each.

Plastic double trophies. Aviva. Early 1970s. $20-30 each.

Plastic trophies. Aviva. Early 1980s.
$10-15 each.

Plastic trophies. Aviva. 1969-
1980s. $10-15 each.

Plastic trophies. Aviva. 1969-1980s.
$10-15 each.

Plastic trophies. Aviva. 1969-1980s. $10-15 each.

Plastic Sparkie figural. Snoopy as the Flying Ace on his house which is on a spring. Aviva. 1971-1972. $30-40.

Ring-A-Ding

Ceramic Charlie Brown bell. 1990. Willitts. 40th Anniversary bell. $30-40.

Ceramic "Beaglescout" bell. Schmid. 1984. $35-40.

Water Land

Snow globes. Comic figures. S.L. Spain. Felicidades on bottom. 4". $50-75 each.

Lucy snow dome. Willitts. 1990.
$25-30.

Eggs Up

Ceramic Snoopy banks. "Cool Cash".
Willitts. 3". 1990. $15-20 "Surprise a friend
with a hug" & "I feel free." Determined.
1976. $20-30. Snoopy laying in egg.
Determined. Late 1970s. $25-35.

Ceramic eggs. Aviva. Early
1970s. 2-1/2". $25-35
each.

Ceramic egg cups. England. Unknown year. 2-1/2". $20-30 each.

Fun, Fun, Fun Figures

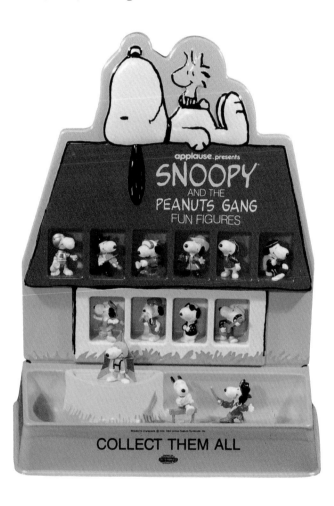

Hula dancing Lucy PVC figure. Applause. Early 1990s. $4-6 each.

Snoopy with Woodstock coming out of package, PVC figure. Applause. Early 1990s. $4-6.

PVC figures. Applause. 1990. $5-7 each.

Lets Play, Charlie Brown

Lionel handcars. Made for a short time. Early 1990s. $150-200 each.

Plastic educational toy. See 'N Say. Mattel. 1969. $75-100.

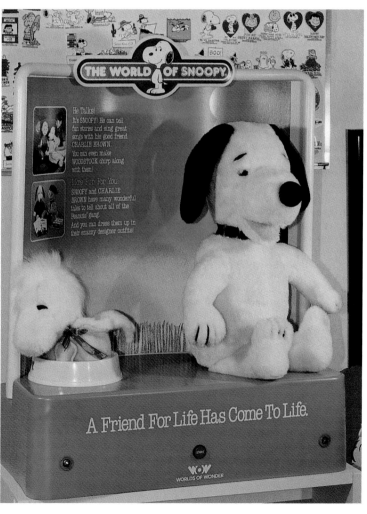

Talking Snoopy display. Worlds of Wonder. Plays different tapes and Snoopy talks and sings. His mouth moves. Woodstock not included in this display. Electric with cardboard background with sensor. 23" x 29" x 13". 1986. $200-300.

Metal Peanuts Talking Bus in original box. (When button on top is pressed the Gang sings and speaks. This bus is a difficult item to find. Most, even in mint condition, can't work because a rubber band is part of the mechanism and is subject to breakage or dry rot. Box or no box, mint or less than is simply a must-have toy. J. Chein & Co. Late 1960s. $250-450.

Die cast metal bus. Peanuts Gang looking out the windows. Snoopy and Woodstock on top of bus. 7-1/2" x 3". Ertl. 1997. $30-40.

Snoopy plastic phonograph. Vanity Fair. Plain white except for inside decal and box. Late 1970s. Topstove Industries. $65-85.

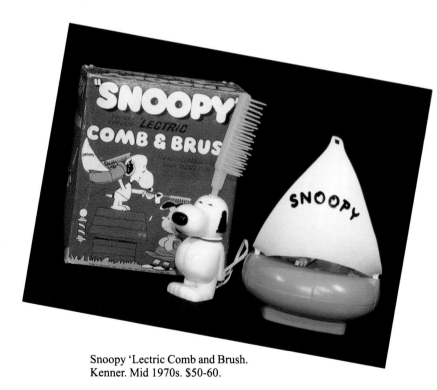

Snoopy 'Lectric Comb and Brush. Kenner. Mid 1970s. $50-60.

64

Plastic Snoopy Drive-In Movie Theater. Kenner. Mid 1970s. $130-170.

Snoopy's Dream Machine! Laminated cardboard Snoopy on doghouse chasing the Red Baron. Lighted action. Late 1970s. $80-120.

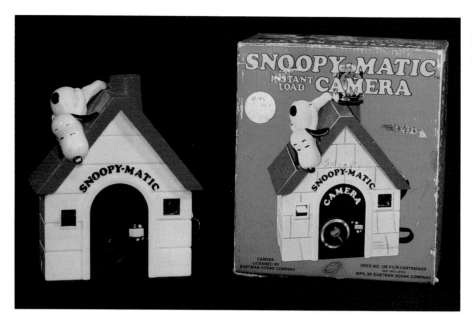

Plastic Snoopy-Matic Camera with original box.
Utilizes 110 film. Helm Toy Co. Late 1970s.
$100-150 with box.

View-Master in box from Gaf.
Late 1970s. $40-60.

View-Master cartoon stereo
images to be viewed with
View-Master. Late 1970s.
$15-25 set.

Wooden Peanuts piano. Ely. Late 1960s. $150-175.

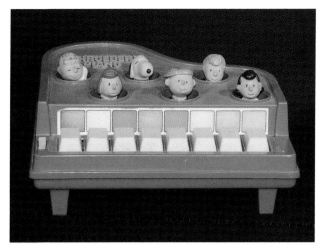

Plastic Schroeder piano. The rubber heads pop up and down when the keys are pressed. Child Guidance. Mid 1970s. $100-125.

Battery-operated Schroeder plastic piano. ITT. 1990s. $50-60. Color variations.

Peanuts Gang metal drum. Chein. Mid 1970s. $75-100 with box.

Peanuts Parade metal drum with wooden sticks. 1960s. Chein & Co. $100-150.

Plastic phone that plays records. Mattel. 1970s. $100-125 in box.

Plastic yo-yo. Hallmark. Early 1970s. $40-50.

Yo-yo string in original waxed bag. Hallmark. 1970s. Blue, green, orange, red characters on package. $10-15 each.

Plastic yo-yos. Hallmark. 1970s. $30-40 in package.

Plastic Joe Cool yo-yo. Late 1970s. Most likely Hallmark. $10-40 fair to mint condition in package.

Peanuts Magic Catch puppets. Plastic head hand puppet with cloth body, velcro hands for catching the ball. Each sold individually with ball in box. Mid 1980s. $20-30.

Lucy, Peanuts push puppet. Plastic. Press underside and characters will wiggle. Ideal. Late 1970s. $20-30.

Charlie Brown plastic push puppet. Push bottom and he wiggles. Ideal. Late 1970s. $20-30.

Snoopy and Woodstock On Skis Balance Toy. Aviva. Not shown: Snoopy and biplane and Snoopy and Woodstock scouting. Late 1970s. Blister pak. $30-45.

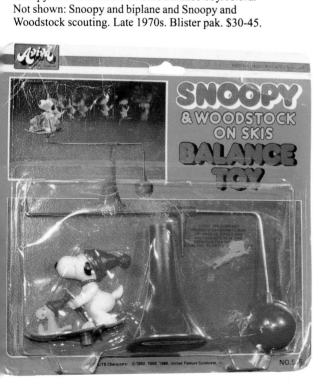

Charlie Brown and Woodstock on skis balance toy. Aviva. Late 1970s. Blister pak. $30-45.

Snoopy and Woodstock on doghouse balancing toy. Aviva. Late 1970s. Blister pak. $30-45.

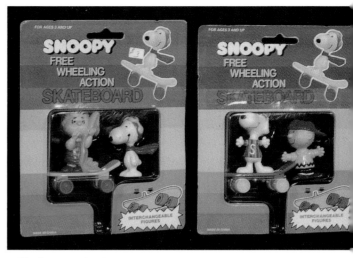

Plastic Free Wheeling Action Skateboard with interchangeable figures. Aviva. Early 1980s. $7-9.

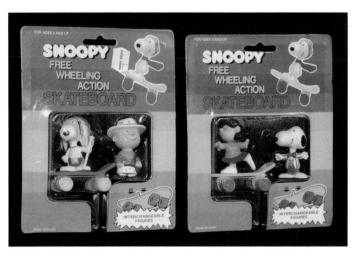

Plastic Free Wheeling Action Skateboard with interchangeable figures. Aviva. Early 1980s. $7-9.

Charlie Brown on skateboard. ITT. 1990s. $5-7 in package.

Plastic Snoopy Snippers. (scissors). Mattel. Mid 1970s. $30-40 with box.

70

Matchbox. radio controlled skateboard. 15" x 13". Uses eight AA batteries and one 9 volt battery. Mid 1990s. $50-75.

Snoopy's Fantastic Automatic Bubble Pipe. Chemtoy. Late 1970s. Plastic pipe shrink wrapped with bottle of bubbles. $15-30.

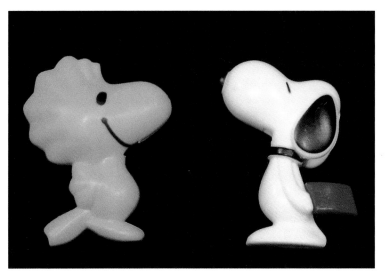

Woodstock and Snoopy plastic whistles. Hallmark. Late 1970s. Came in packages separately. $40-60 each in package. $15-30 each-no package.

Plastic walkers in packages from Aviva. Mid 1970s. $5-7 each.

Plastic rollable, Lucy and Snoopy toys. Aviva. Late 1970s. $6-8 each.

Plastic Charlie Brown toy. Motorized. Aviva. Late 1970s. $20-30 with box.

Wooden train. All American Express. Snoopy Express mechanical wind up train. Aviva. Late 1970s. $40-90.

Plastic Snoopy & Charlie Brown Para-troopers. Late 1980s. $4-6 each.

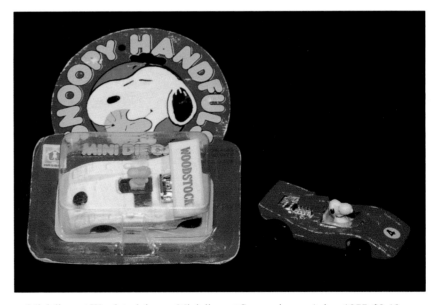

Mini die cast Woodstock in car. Mini die cast Snoopy in car. Aviva. 1977. $8-18 each.

Die cast race cars. Aviva. Late 1970s. $8-15 each.

Die cast race cars. Aviva. late 1970s. $8-15 each.

Happy Die Cast cars with oversized characters. Early 1980s. Hasbro. $10-15 each.

Mini die cast wagons. Aviva. Late 1970s. With package. $15-20 each.

Charlie Brown and Snoopy plastic toy shoes. ITT. Early 1990s. $3-5 each.

Die cast car with Peanuts gang.
Aviva. Late 1970s. Plastic trim.
Almost 5". $25-65 fair to mint
in package.

Plastic friction vehicles. Late
1970s. Aviva. Characters are
rubber. Snoopy in house most
common. $15-40 each.

Charlie Brown, part of a train. Aviva.
1970s. $10-40.

Plastic Flying Ace toy. Aviva. Late
1970s. Probably part of a train.
$10-40 mint.

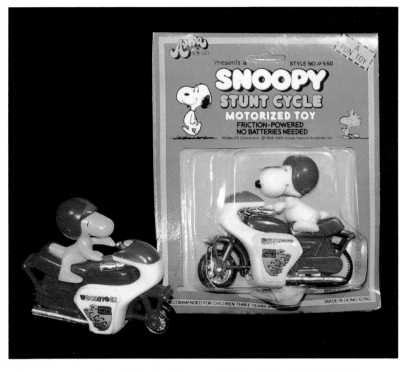

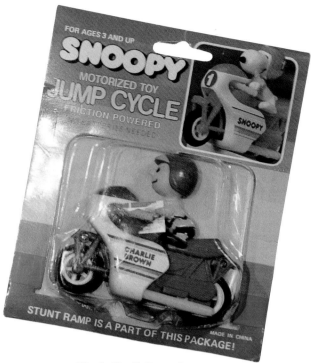

Snoopy stunt cycle and Woodstock stunt cycle from Aviva. 1980s. $10-15.

Plastic Charlie Brown jump friction motorcycle. ITT. 1990s. $7-10.

Cardboard kaleido-scope. Hallmark. 1970s. $18-25.

Rubber Peanuts Gang figures. No marks or date. $5- 6 each.

Rubber finger puppets. Ideal. Determined. Showtime. $7-9. 8 different available but not shown. Snoopy, Linus, Sally, Schroeder, Woodstock, Peppermint Patty. Late 1970s.

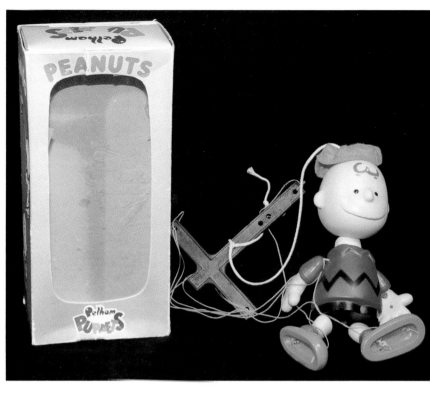

Woodstock puppet, plastic with felt wings and bill.
Peanuts, Pelham Puppet. Made in England. Late 1970s.
$50-75.

Charlie Brown puppet by Pelham Co. of England. 1979. $75-100.

Lucy, Charlie Brown & Snoopy rubber Skediddlers. Mattel. Late 1960s.
$30-45. Items pictured were sold individually. Peanuts Skediddler Club
House Set also sold together in package. 1970. $75-100.

Rubber Linus Skediddler. Mattel.
Late 1960s. $30- 45.

76

Snoopy Skediddler vinyl case with inside view. Case made in various colors. Mattel. Late 1960s. $125-175 in box.

Tin dish set with paper napkins, plastic tea pot and utensils. Chein. This set is window boxed. Early 1970s. $150-175 with box.

Tea set contains metal dishes with plastic cups and toaster. Ohio Art. Late 1980s. $25-35.

Tea set contains metal dishes with plastic cups, utensils and tea pot. Ohio Art. Late 1980s. $25-35.

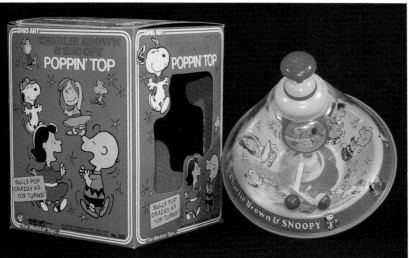

Charlie Brown and Snoopy Poppin' Top. Ohio Art 1980. $30-45.

Metal spinning top, original box.
Ohio Art. 1980s. $20-30.

Metal Peanuts spinning top.
Chein. Japan. Late 1960s.
$80-100.

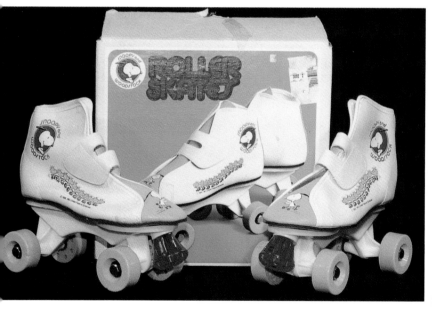

Child's Snoopy roller skates. Nash. Vinyl. 1980s. $25-30.

Plastic Snoopy Jack-in-the box.
Romper Room/Hasbro. Early
1980s. $20-25.

79

Woodstock pop up plastic toy from Aviva.
1970s. $7-12.

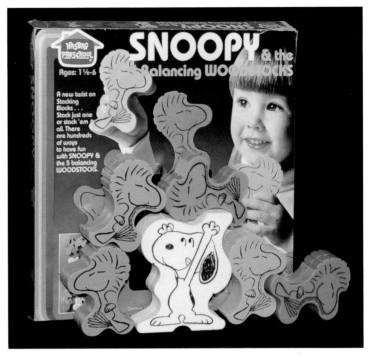

Snoopy & the Balancing Woodstocks. Hasbro/Pre- school. Late 1980s.
$15-20.

Plastic Peanuts License Plate for bicycles.
Hallmark. 1980s. $6-10 each in package.

Bicycle spoke reflectors. Lucy on bike with
Snoopy. Hallmark. 1980s. $8-10.

Plastic bicycle baskets with plastic Joe Cool on front. 1980s/90s. Also available in pink. $6-9.

Drew Porges holding a pair of Snoopy Ski School, skis. Nash Manufacturing "trainers" taught youngsters how to ski. Wooden. 48". 1980s. $30-40.

Plastic Snoopy Bike Valve Caps. Bikway. Early 1980s. $15-20.

Inflatable Peanuts gang pool. Intex. Early 1990s. $25-35 mint in box.

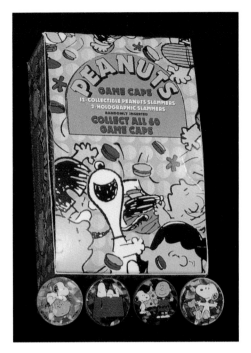

Display box for game caps. Pogs and
slammers. Individually wrapped pack
contains 6 pogs and slammers. American
Game Corp. 1990s. $4-6 each pack.

Super Star collectors cards. Preview
edition. Tuff Stuff. 1992. $17-22 each.
Also made in French and Spanish and an
uncut version.

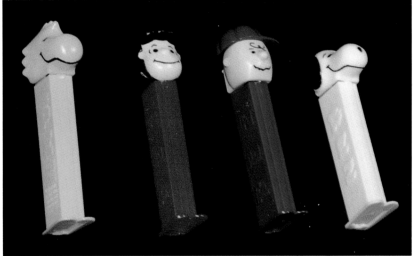

Plastic Pez candy
containers. 1990s. $1-4.

Tin Space Patrol Snoopy.
Unlicenced but still sought
after. Unknown maker,
1980? $150-175.

Inflatable Snoopy blimp. 1990s.
$12-18 in package.

Rubber Peanuts Gang dog
toys. Con Agra Pet Prod-
ucts. 1990s. $3-5 each.

Plastic dog dish. Determined.
Came in 5" and 7" sizes. 1970s.
$10-20.

Rubber Snoopy in boat floating
squeaky toy. Unknown maker.
1980s. $4-6.

83

Puzzle Me This, Linus

Peanuts Mini jigsaw puzzle. Full figure Snoopy walking. Part of a set. 5-1/4" x 7". Milton Bradley. Early 1970s. $7-10.

Wooden puzzle from Playskool. Snoopy kissing Lucy. 9.5" x 11.5". 1980s. $10-15

3 mini, Milton Bradley, puzzles. Early 1970s. $7-10 each.

3 mini, Milton Bradley, puzzles. Early 1970s. $7-10 each.

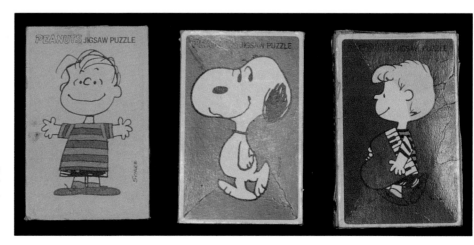

Cardboard Peanuts puzzles. Golden. 1980s/
90s. $4-6 each.

Peanuts Gang puzzle from Milton Bradley.
1980s. $6-10.

The Gang boating puzzle. Milton
Bradley. 1980s. $6-10.

Linus puzzle from Milton Bradley. 1970s. $7-18.

Cardboard Peanuts Gang puzzle. Springbrook. Early 1990s. $10-15.

Peanuts Gang, at the park, puzzle. Springbrook/Hallmark. 1980s. $10-15.

The Gang playing baseball puzzle. Springbrook. 1980s. $10-15.

Lucy cardboard puzzle. Springbrook.
1980s. $5-7.

Interlocking puzzle with the Peanuts Gang. Springbrook/
Hallmark. Late 1980s early 90s. $10-12.

Peanuts Gang puzzle. "No dogs allowed." Golden.
1980-90s. $4-6.

Peanuts Gang puzzle. Golden.
1980s-90s. $4-6.

A Charlie Brown Christmas Family Puzzle. 1996. Hallmark/Springbrook. Commemorating 30th anniversary of "A Charlie Brown Christmas." $15-20.

Peanuts family puzzle. (Hallmark photographed, Pauline Graber's favorite things.) 1995. $15-20.

Peanuts Gang matchbox puzzles. 10pc's. 1980s. $3-7 each.

Gametime

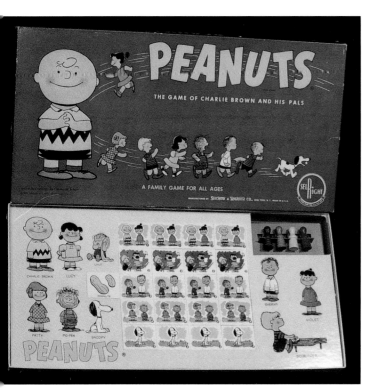

Peanuts Game. Selchow & Richter. Late 1960s. $45-60.

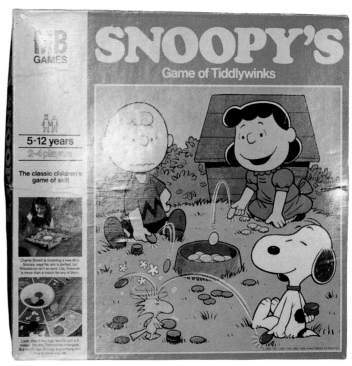

Snoopy's Game of Tiddlywinks.
Milton Bradley, 1970s. $20-25.

The Pursuit of Happiness Game. Early
1970s. Determined. $40-50.

Game cards. Hallmark. Mid 1970s.
$15-25 each, good to mint.

Snoopy Game from Milton
Bradley. 1970s. $15-25.

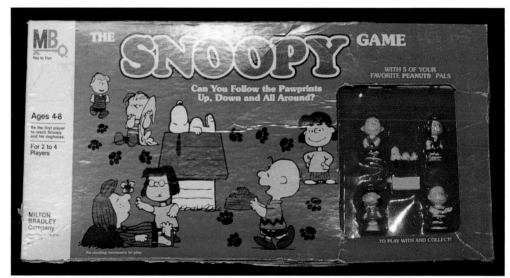

Snoopy Card Game from Milton
Bradley. Mid 1970s. $20-25.

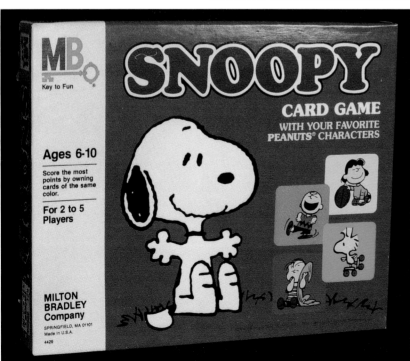

Plastic Picture Maker. Mattel. Early 1970s. $35-45.

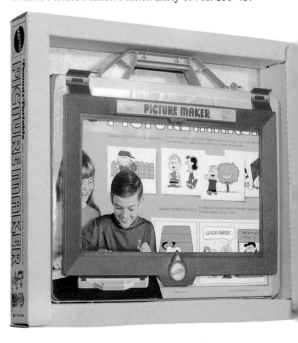

Lucy's Tea Party Game from Milton Bradley. Early
1970s. $40-50.

Plastic pin ball machine. "Can you catch it, Cnarlie
Brown?" Ideal. Mid 1970s. $100-125.

Charlie Brown's All Stars game by Parker Bros. Mid 1970s. $30-40.

Great Shakes, Charlie Brown! Dice game.
1990s. Made by Golden. $10-15.

91

Dollworld and Pillowtalk

Rubber Hungerford Peanut Gang set. 1958. Hungerford Plastics. This particular set is mint. The only thing that could ever value them more is a cello wrap with a cartoon panel top. Very rare to find mint in package. The clothing is painted on these dolls. The smaller version is more valued than the standard; Schroeder with the coveted piano being the very most difficult to locate. 8.5" Lucy, 8.5" Charlie Brown, 7" Snoopy, 8.5" Linus with blanket not attached, $30-90. 8.5" Pig Pen $75-125. 6" Baby Sally, $75- 125. 7" Schroeder with piano, $200-300. 7.25" Lucy, 7.5" Charlie Brown, 5.5" Snoopy 60-150 each. Standard set in good condition $700-800.

Lucy, Snoopy, Charlie Brown. Plastic articulated dolls. Determined. 1970s. $25-50.

Rubber Playables. Lucy. Determined. Late 1960s. $5-30 with package.

Rubber Playables. Snoopy, Charlie Brown and Linus. Flat with clothing painted on. Determined. 1960s. $5-30. Most costly mint in package.

Peanuts Gang pocket dolls from Boucher. Missing Lucy with smile. Late 1960s. $15-25 each.

Dress Me Belle with wardrobe. Each bought separately. Knickerbocker. 1983. Dolls $35-45 each. Outfits, mint in package. $10-15 each.

Dress Me Belle doll. Belle came with signature pink dress. This old fashioned outfit (hat missing) would have been purchase separately on a card. Belle doll in box is most valued. $15-40. Outfits on cards. 1983. $10-15.

Snoopy with earphones. Determined. Early 1980s. $15-40. Depending on condition.

Knickerbocker vinyl Snoopy and Belle
dolls. 8". 1983. $35-45 each.

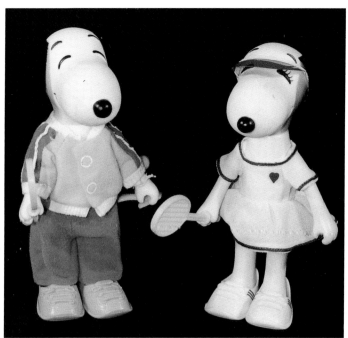

Knickerbocker vinyl Snoopy and Belle dolls. 8". 1983. $35-45 each.

Knickerbocker vinyl Snoopy and
Belle dolls. 8". 1983. $35-45 each.

Plush Linus holding blanket and sucking
thumb. 1980s. Determined. 7". $20-30.

Plush Charlie, Lucy, Peppermint Patty dolls. Clothing is removable. Determined. 1980s. $20-30 each. Linus is not shown.

Peanuts gang. Clothing is not removable. 1980s. Determined. $20-30 each.

Plastic Peanuts Gang dolls with stands. 1990. 40th Anniversary. Each sold separately. Determined. Doll stands. $6-9 each. Doll $25-35 each.

Dolls. McDonalds premiums. Bought separately. Japan. Mid 1990s. $15-20 each $75 set.

Plush and velour Peanut gang clip on figures. Determined. 1980s. $7-10 each.

Worlds of Wonder talking Snoopy and Woodstock. 1980s. Place tape in Snoopy and he will read to you out of various books. He also has various outfits to wear. Press Woodstock's sides and he chirps. Outfit was sold separately. Snoopy with box $75-100. Outfit $15-20. Book complete with tape. $10-15. Woodstock with box $20-25.

Plush Snoopy PJ bag/Commonwealth Toy & Novelty Co. Zipper on stomach. 2 sizes both 16"; one is larger in diameter. One has Woodstock emblem on chest. $15-20.

Plush Snoopy as Mr. S. Big T Enterprises Inc. 12". Fashioned after Mr. T. from the TV series "A-Team." Early 1980s. $60-75 in box.

Plush Snoopy and Belle. Special edition, commemorating the Olympic year 1984 that Levi Straus clothed the human athletes and canines. Determined. $50-75 each.

Plush sitting Snoopy. Determined. Early 1970s. Notice plastic tag on 15" size. Paper tag on 12" size. Also signature black spot on back. Large $25-35. Small $15-25.

Plush Belle gymnast. She has legs that are stiff so she stands alone. Early 1980s. Determined. $30-35.

Plush Flashbeagle, stands on own stiff legs. Determined. 1980. $30-40.

Plush Belle and Snoopy bride and groom. Applause. Early 1990s. $20-25 each. $45-55 set.

Plush Woodstock with Easter egg. Applause. 1990s. $12-18.

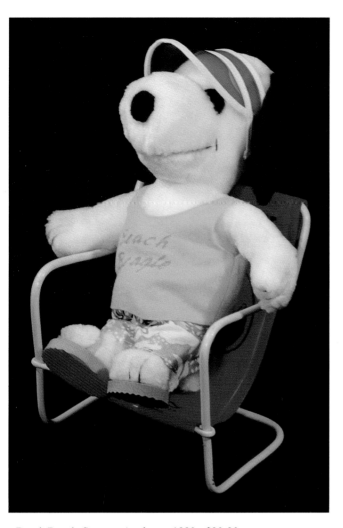

Beach Beagle Snoopy. Applause. 1990s. $20-30.

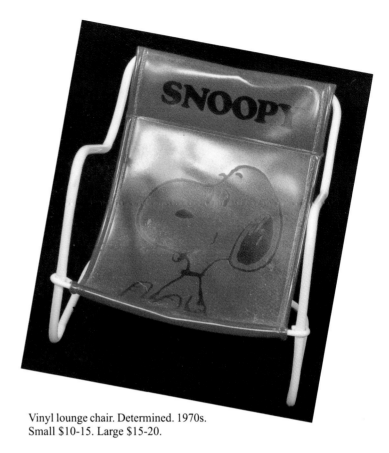

Vinyl lounge chair. Determined. 1970s. Small $10-15. Large $15-20.

Plush Daisy Hill puppies. Determined. Came in various sizes. 6"-$7-10 each. 12"- $15-20 each. 18"-$20-25 each. 1995. They were sold individually. Snoopy, Spike, Belle, Andy, Marbles, Olaf. (Daisy Hill puppy farm is where Charlie Brown bought Snoopy.) Dakin later made these puppies for Determined. Around the same time these puppies were released, a book "Mischief on Daisy Hill" by Determined, and a movie "Snoopy's Reunion" by Paramount were released.

Beach Beagle Belle. Applause. Early 1990s. $20- 30.

Plush Spike stuffed toy. One of Daisy Hill Puppies. Dakin. Mid 1990s. $20-25.

Plush Belle, Snoopy's sister, stuffed toy. Applause. Early 1990s. $15-20.

Plush, stuffed Belle doll. Determined. 1980s. $20- 25 with outfit.

Plush sitting Spike, Snoopy's brother. Determined. Late 1970s. $20-25.

Plush Snoopy Notre Dame. 1980s-90s. $15-20.

Cotton Christmas Snoopy and Belle. Bought individually. Each came wrapped in a plastic bag with red hook/tie closure. Determined. Late 1980s. $15-20 each. $45-50 set mint.

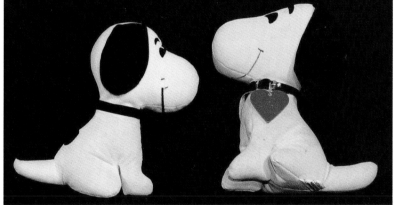

Velour sitting Snoopys. Comic strip Heart says, "Official dog from Peanuts" /flip side "I love you". 1970s. 6" & 8". $5-15.

Fabric Snoopy magician. Ideal. 1970s. 14". $75- 135.

Machine washable Snoopy baby. Dakin. 1996-97. $12-15.

Terry cloth Belle stuffed baby toy. Determined. Late 1980s. $10-12.

Baby wrist rattles with original display box. Machine washable. Dakin. 1996-97. $6-8 each.

Charlie Brown in his box. Applause. 1990s. $7-10 each.

Cotton stuffed Lucy inside cardboard stand. Applause. 1990. $6-8.

Cloth greeting figures. Applause. 4"-6" tall. 1990. $5-7 each.

Box with cloth Woodstock by Applause. 1990s. $7-10.

Cotton Lucy and Charlie rag dolls, Ideal. Removable clothes. 1976. $20-35 each.

Putt Pups Snoopy and Belle skate cotton stuffed shoes. Applause. Other styles available. 1990s. $20-25.

Cotton Lucy and Charlie Brown dolls. Determined. 1980s. $15-20 each.

Needlepoint mini Charlie Brown pillow/ wall hanging. 5". 1970s. Malina. $6-8.

Cotton stuffed Belle, learning toy. Determined. Late 1980s/90s. $20-25.

Needlepoint Snoopy and Woodstock pillow. Made from kit. Malina. 1970s. $40-60 as shown. Mint kit $25-35.

Cotton Schroeder, Linus, Lucy, Charlie Brown, pillow doll. These dolls were all stuffed with kapok, clothing is printed on. Late 1960s. Determined. Also available not shown. Snoopy playing baseball. 14"-18". $10-30 each.

Mini pillow, Freida and Snoopy. Unknown maker and era-or if handmade. $3-4.

Belle stuffed pillow. FCI, 1980. 13". $7-10..

Cotton stuffed dolls of Sally , Lucy and Linus. FCI. 6". Cut/stitch/stuff cloth. Early 1980s. $2-4 each. Charlie Brown and Snoopy are not shown.

Welcome to Our Playroom

(Joe) Cool Furniture Man!

Hard board top/stainless steel frame. Table and chair set. Late 1980s/90s. $90-125.

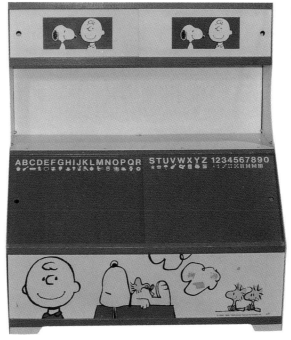

Wooden toy chest with sliding doors. Late 1980s early 1990s. $70-100.

Wooden Snoopy and Charlie Brown hutch. Unknown maker. Early 1990s. $60-85.

Snoopy & Co. storage box. 15.5". 1988. Trojan Luggage company. $40-50.

Snoopy Playhouse for indoors or out. Intex. 1990. $30-40 in box. It is shown set up below left.

Metal waste can with the Peanuts Gang. Chein. Early 1970s. $20-30.

Ashley Lindenberger (author's grand daughter) sitting by Snoopy Playhouse.

Metal waste can with Charlie Brown, Lucy, Snoopy. Chein. Early 1970s. $20-30. Reverse side says "Charlie Brown. Good grief, I'm a star!".

Metal Linus waste paper can. 1970s. Chein. $25-35.

Metal waste basket. Chein. Early 1970s.
$20-30 depending on condition.

Tin Peanuts Gang waste can with plastic lid.
Doubles as a stool. Late 1980s. PNK Products.
$30-35.

Metal waste paper can. Seat combination.
PNK Products. Late 1980s. $30-35.

Metal waste paper can. Seat combination.
PNK Products. Late 1980s. $30-35.

Hung Up on You, Lucy

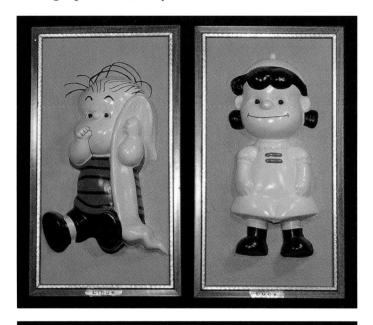

Wood plaque. Hallmark. Late 1980s. $10-15.

Lucy and Linus, Snoopy and Charlie three dimensional plastic framed pictures. 8" x 14". Late 1960s. $30-35 each.

Peanuts Gang mirror. Determined made in England. Mid 1970s. $30-35.

Wall plaques. Hallmark. 1970s/80s. $10-15 each.

Wooden decoupage Peanuts picture. A Boy named Charlie Brown, the first Peanuts movie. $10-15.

Poster of Snoopy surfing. Large size. Hallmark. 1970s. $10-12.

Mirror, London bus and Peanuts Gang. 13" x 9". Determined. England. Mid 1970s. $35-45.

Embroidered Peanuts Gang picture. Made from a kit. Malina. Mid 1970s. $20-25.

Chicago Tribune full page pull out page.

Chicago Tribune full page. Chicago Tribune. In 1968 the Chicago Tribune published 12 full page Peanuts Gang posters. They were published weekly and in color. They are now very rare individually & even more so as a complete set. $25-35 each or $400-500 set.

Snoopy poster and pen set. Craft House. Five non-toxic pens with one 12" x 16" paper poster and one 12" x 16"' poster board. Early 1990s. $12-17 complete.

40 Years of Happiness. 1990. Hallmark gave this poster away free with purchase. $5-8 each.

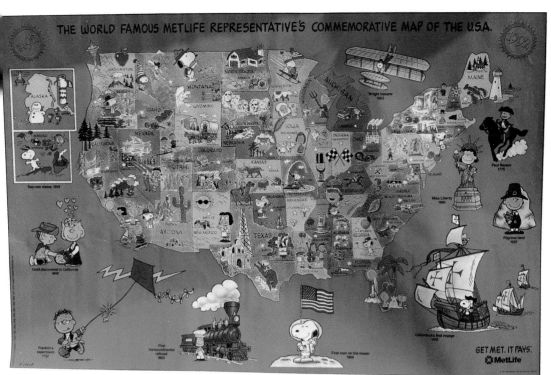

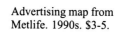

Advertising map from Metlife. 1990s. $3-5.

Yesteryears. A celebration of the Golden Era of television and radio. Commemorative of 40 years of Peanuts. Winter. 1990. $4-5.

Lucy mini poster. 1980s. $3-5.

Original comic strip signed by Charles Schulz. This is a highly prized collectible. Especially autographed. Weekly strips valued at $1000-1200. Sunday strips valued at $2000-2700. Age is also a factor of value, for example, Snoopy walking on all four legs, is highly valued.

"A Boy Named Charlie Brown," movie still. 1969. $10- 15.

Ceramic Snoopy on doghouse wall plaque. 1980s. One of a set including entire gang of characters. $25-35.

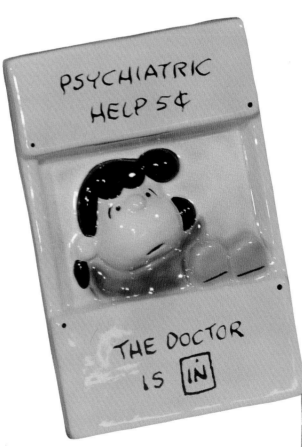

Ceramic wall plaque. Lucy at lemonade stand. 1980s. Included in same set as Snoopy on yellow house. $25-35.

Room decorating kit. Jumbo appliques. 3M Co. Early 1990s. $30-40.

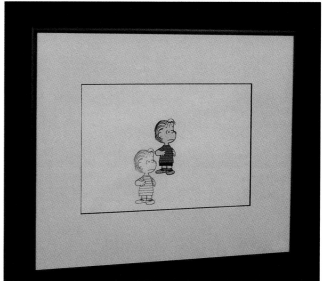

The Peanut gang cels. Probably 1970s. Single figures with pencil sketch background. One character $350-400, Two characters $400-500. Prices include matting and frames.

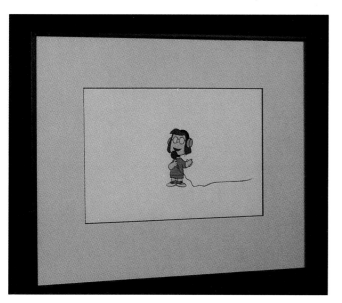

Cel of Linus and Peppermint Patty with color background. $750-900.

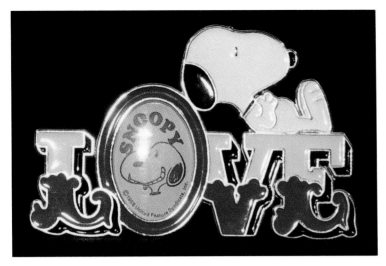

Metal picture frame. Butterfly. 1979. $30-40.

Charlie Brown and Snoopy metal picture
frame. 1980s. $15-20.

Metal picture frame. Snoopy holding balloons. Enameled.
Butterfly. Late 1970s. $20-25.

Silverplate picture frame from
Godinger. 1990s. $25-30.

Cotton Flying Ace wall hanging. Silgo. Early 1990s. $30-40.

Linen tea towel. Determined. Mid 1970s. $20-25.

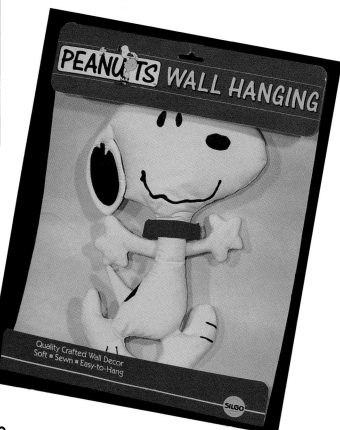

Cotton Snoopy wall hanging from Silgo. Early 1990s. $20-30.

Cork bulletin board. Mid 1970s. $20-30 large poster size. Probably Manton.

Snoopy and Woodstock cork bulletin board. Plastic frame. Manton Cork Co. 1980s. Possible late 1970s. 24" x 18". $20-25.

Cork bulletin board. Manton. Early 1980s. $20-30 depending on condition.

Peanuts gang cork bulletin board. Manton Cork Corp. 1980s. $15-25.

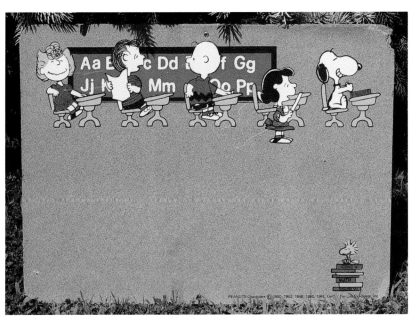

Plastic thermometer. Sybron/
Taylor. Early 1980s. $7-10.

Cork Peanuts Gang note board. Manton Cork Co. 1980s. $15-25.

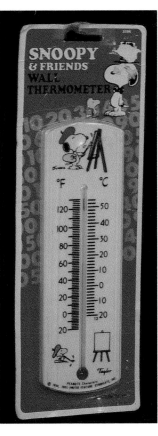

Wooden thermometer. Taylor,
USA. 5" x 24". Late 1970s.
$45-60.

Thermometer. Sybron/Taylor.
Early 1980s. $15-20.

Felt banner. Determined. 1970. $15-20.

Felt pennant. "A Boy Named Charlie Brown" by Determined Prod. 1970s. $15-20.

Felt Linus banner. 1970s. Determined Prod. $15-25.

Felt Snoopy banner. Early. 1970s. $20-25.

Felt Snoopy banner. Early 1970s. $20-25.

Felt Lucy banner. Determined. Early 1970s. Character banners being more rare than Snoopy. $20-30.

Professional major league team pennants. Early 1990s. $5-7 each.

Professional major league team pennants. Early 1990s. $5-7 each.

Glass one piece table lamp. 9". From Japan. Unknown maker. $100-125.

Plastic Snoopy on doghouse night light. Hallmark. 1980s. $20-40 mint to fair.

Ceramic Snoopy desk lamp. C.N. Burman Co. Late 1980s early 90s. $30-40 with box.

Glass light globe with the Peanuts Gang. 1990s. $20-25.

Peanuts Gang Japanese lantern. 1990s. $15-20.

Plastic switch plate from Hallmark. 1980s. $8-12.

Ceiling fan and light kit. Sports variation. Also available "Fan for all Seasons." Each blade has Snoopy doing activities relevant to each season. Sisco Inc. 1980s. $75-125.

Snoopy alarm clock. Citizen. Japan. 1990s. $20-25.

Plastic switch plate from Hallmark. 1970s. $12-15.

Large alarm clock with Charlie Brown, Snoopy and Woodstock by Salton. 1990s. $40-50.

Plastic Charlie Brown and Snoopy talking clock by Equity. Talking alarm. Late 1970s. $150-175.

Pigpen, Don't Wipe Your Feet on These, Please

Latch hook Peanuts rug or wall hanging. Malina. Mid 1970s. $30-40 mint in box.

Latch hook Snoopy and Woodstock rug/wall hanging. Made from kit. Malina. Mid 1970s. 20" x 27". Completed as shown. $40-50 mint in box. $30-40 as shown.

Latch hook Charlie Brown rug/wall hanging. Made from kit. Malina. 15" x 16". Mid 1970s. Completed as shown. $20-25. Mint in box. $25-35.

Latch hook Lucy rug from Malina Co. Made from a kit, 20" x 27". 1970s. $40-50 mint in box, $30-40 as shown.

Latch hook Sally rug/wall hanging. Made from kit. Malina. Mid 1970s. 15" x 15". Completed as shown. $20-25. Mint in box. $25-35.

In the 1990s, Frank T. Greco Inc. produced a large reasonably priced selection of cotton throw rugs that could be utilized for floor or wall decoration. These high quality handmade and individually screen printed rugs came in various sizes with different scenes depicted. 22" x 40" and 20" x 34".

Cotton Peanuts Gang rug. Frank T. Greco. 1990s. $15-25.

Cotton Snoopy in Gondola with Woodstock rug. Frank T. Greco. 1990s. $15-25.

Rubber door mat. Snoopy and Woodstock. Determined Productions. 1980s-90s. $15-20.

Pay Attention in School, Peppermint Patty

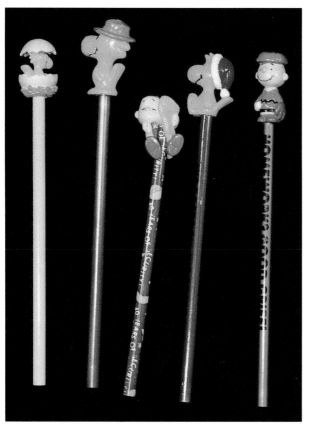

Decorated pencils. 1990s. Applause. $3-4 each.

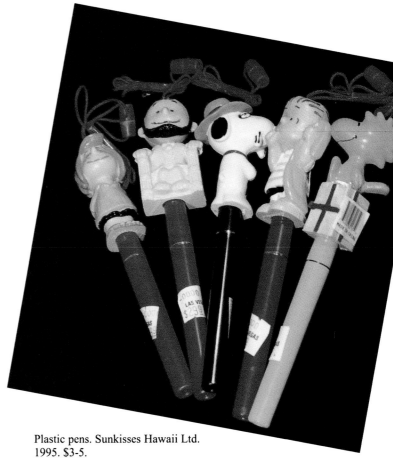

Plastic pens. Sunkisses Hawaii Ltd.
1995. $3-5.

Plastic pens. Sunkisses
Hawaii. Ltd. 1995. $3-5 each.

Cardboard display box for Peanuts pens. Sunkisses Hawaii Ltd. Mid 1990s. $5-7.

Gold tone Peanuts ball point pen. Linus with blanket. Stylus. Mid 1990s. $30-35.

Metal ruler. $3-6.

Gold tone Peanuts ball point pens. Woodstock and Lucy. (Linus tag does not go with Woodstock pen) Stylus. Mid 1990s. Commemorative 45th anniversary of Peanuts collectors tin. $30-35 each.

Peanuts ball point pens. Snoopy on doghouse and sitting Snoopy. Gold tone. 45th anniversary of Peanuts collector tin. Stylus. $30-35 each.

Plastic Snoopy ruler. Hallmark. Probably 1980s. $7-10.

Metal magnetic Peanuts bulletin board. 1990s. Collectible board. $7-12 Magnets are from different makers.

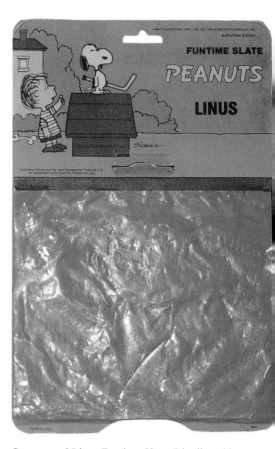

Snoopy and Linus Funtime Slate. Distributed by Aero Educational Products Ltd. in co-operation with Child Art Products, Inc. 1970s. $7-10.

Clip board. Spike. Butterfly. Early 1980s. $7-10.

Brite Writer Magic Slate. Golden. 1980s/90s. $3-4.

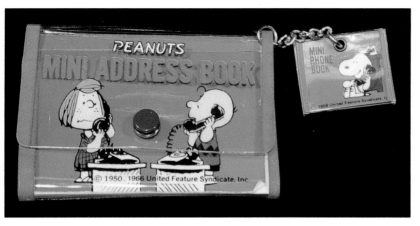

Mini Peanuts Address Book. Butterfly. Early 1980s. $6-8.

Lucy Diary from Hallmark. 1980s. $12-15.

Mini telephone book. Butterfly. Early 1980s. $4-6.

Peanuts memo pads. Older. Possibly Hallmark. $5-8 each.

Peanuts memo book and Snoopy autograph books. Butterfly. Early 1980s. $12-17.

Peanuts Date Book (calendar). Different picture on each page. Determined. 1968. $10-15.

Marcie's Library

Calender computer program with bonus wrist pad. Make your own calender with Peanuts from now to eternity. 1992. Individual Software. $30-40

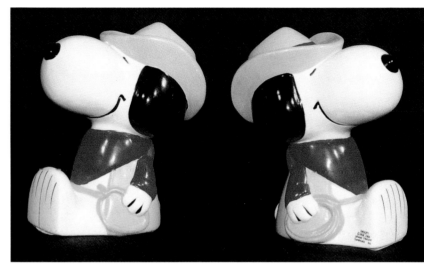

Cowboy Snoopy ceramic bookends. Butterfly. 1979. 5". $60-75.

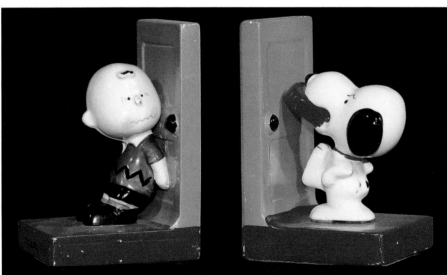

Ceramic Snoopy and Charlie Brown bookends. Butterfly. Mid 1970s. $150-200.

Ceramic Snoopy in rain slicker and umbrella bookends. Butterfly. 1979. 5". $60-75.

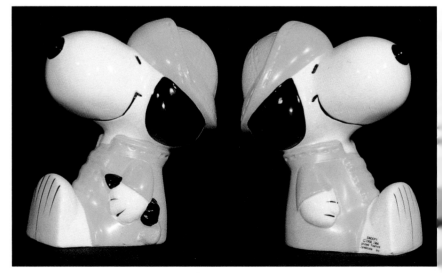

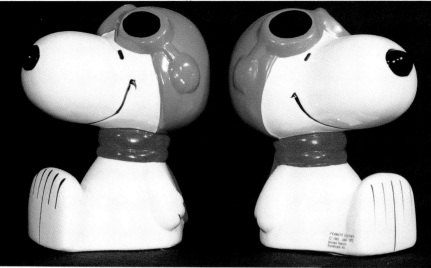

Ceramic Snoopy as Flying Ace bookends. Butterfly. 1979. 5". $60-75.

Ceramic Baseball Snoopy bookends. Butterfly. 5". 1979. $60-75.

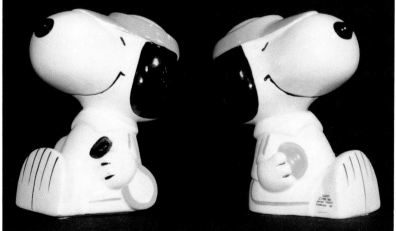

Ceramic Tennis player Snoopy bookends. Butterfly. 5". 1979. 5". $60-75.

Hard rubber Snoopy hugging Woodstock bookend. Butterfly. 1981. $35-45.

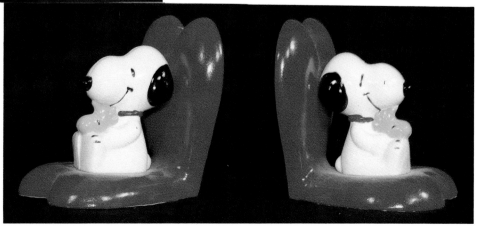

Ceramic Snoopy and locomotive bookends. Willitts. Early 1990s. Train 7" x 6". Caboose 4-1/4" x 4-3/4". $60-75.

Ceramic Snoopy sitting on books, bookends. 5" x 5". Rare. Also came with yellow books. $150-200.

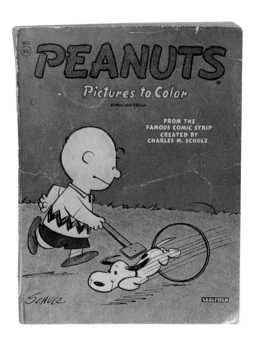

Coloring book. Saalfield, 1960s. $30-40 if mint.

Peanuts *Linus Coloring Book.* Saalfield, 1960s. $25-35.

136

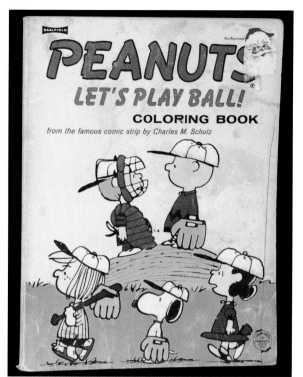

Peanuts coloring book. *Let's Play Ball*. Saalfield. 1967. $25-35.

Peanuts *Lucy Coloring Book*. Saalfield, late 1960s. $25-35.

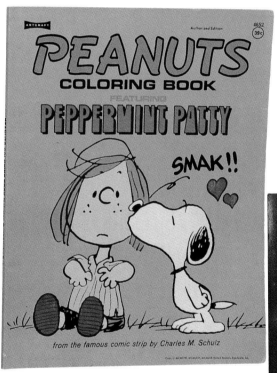

Peanuts coloring books. Saalfield. 1960s. $25-35.

Peanuts Coloring Book. Peppermint Patty. Saalfield. 1972. $25-35.

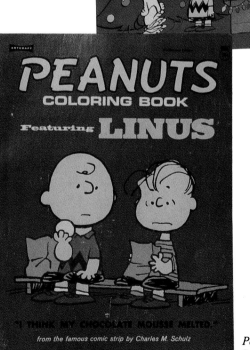

Peanuts Coloring Book. Linus. Saalfield. 1972. $25-35.

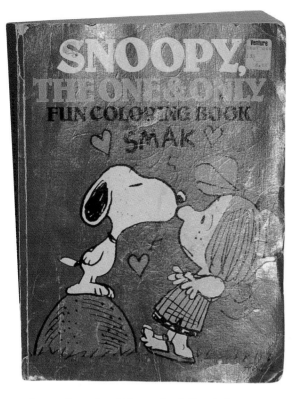

Shapes and Sizes Activity book. Cinnamon House. 1980s. $5-7.

Jack and Jill magazine. Jan. 1977. $8-10.

Snoopy large *Fun Coloring Book.* Ottenheimer Publishers Inc. 1970s. $7-9.

Peanuts and Charlie Brown fun books. Determined. 1980. $15-20 each.

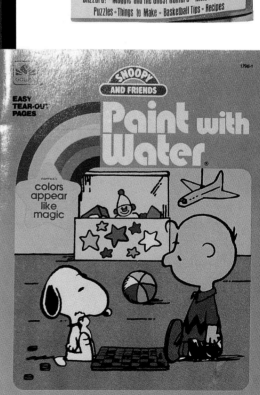

Paint with Water Charlie Brown book. Golden. Late 1980s early 1990s. $2-4 each.

Peanuts Gang coloring books. Happy House. 1984. $3-6 each.

Surprises magazine. Feb. 1972. $10-12.

Mad magazine. Oct. 1970. $10-12.

Family Circle magazine. April, 1969. $10-12.

Time magazine with Peanuts Gang
article. 1986. $10 -12.

Time Magazine with Peanuts article inside. April, 1965. $15-20.

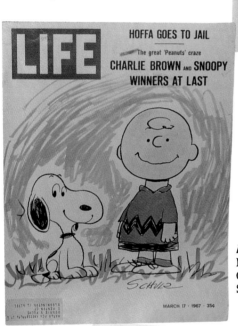

Magazine cover from *Saturday Review* April 1969. $15-20.

Newsweek magazine from December 1971. $10-15.

Life magazine from March 17, 1967 with Charlie Brown and Snoopy article. $9-12.

Notre Dame University program sponsored by Northwest Airlines. Special Olympics Celebrity Hockey Challenge. $5-7.

First of all, lets hash some numbers. There are well over one hundred comic books either dedicated to Peanuts or featuring the Peanuts Gang. While listing issue numbers, please note, these are probably not complete. The Peanuts comics are most valued. The prices listed are mint, very good, no marks. little or no wear. Please be very aware of condition. Date and issue are always on the inside. For more information please refer to the *Overstreet Comic Book Guide*.

Fritz-Ritz Comics. Years published 1952-1958. Issue #22,24,25,26,57,58,59. $20-25 each

Tip Top Comics. Years published 1954-1961. Issue #173,185,225. $20-25 each. Please note Tip Top covers are usually 2-3 panels. Only one features the Peanut Gang. The cover featuring entirely Peanuts is a rare find indeed.

Nancy. Years published 1957-1959. Issue #146-173. $10-15 each

Nancy and Sluggo. Years published 1960-1963. Issue # 174-192. $10-15 each

Fritz-Ritz, Tip Top, Nancy, Nancy and Sluggo only feature 2-6 pages of Peanuts.

Peanuts-Dell Comics. Years published 1958-1962. Issue #1,13,878,969,1015. The first Dell Comics can go for $100. The later Dells $50-100

Peanuts-Gold Key comics after 1963. Reprints of Dell Comics same issue numbers. $10-30 each

Dell 10 cent *Tip Top* comic.

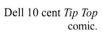

Dell 10 cent *Tip Top* comic.

Dell *Nancy* comic with Snoopy.

Tip Top Peanut comic.

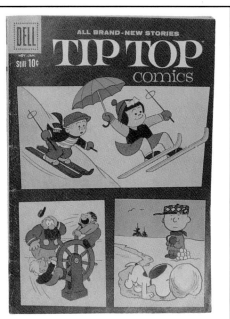

Tip Top 10 cent comics from Dell.

Dell 10 cent comic. *Peanuts.*

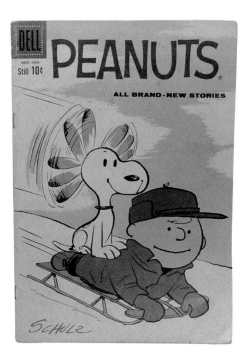

Dell 10 cent comic. *Peanuts.*

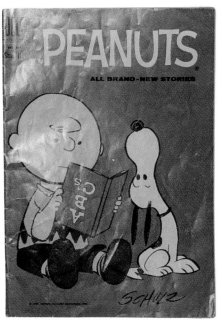

Dell 10 cent comic. *Peanuts.*

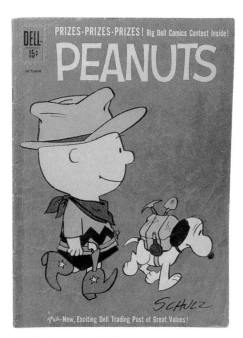

Dell 15 cent comic. *Peanuts.*

Dell 15 cent comic. *Peanuts*.

Dell 15 cent comic. *Peanuts*.

Gold Key *Peanuts* comic.

Dell 15 cent comic. *Peanuts*.

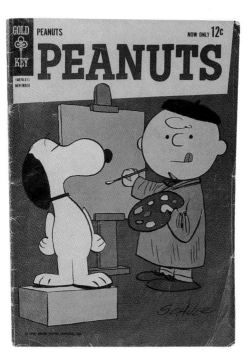

Gold key 12 cent comic. *Peanuts*.

Gold key 12 cent comic. *Peanuts*.

You Can't Vote, Go Fly a Kite, It's a Dog's Life books by Charles Schulz. Soft cover. Holt/Rinehart and Winston. Early 1960s. $8-15 each.

More Peanuts book by Holt, Rinehart and Winston, Inc. Published Sept. 1954. 22nd. printing. 1967. $8-12.

But We Love You, Charlie Brown, late 1950s. *You're You, Charlie Brown*, 1968. *You Need Help, Charlie Brown*, 1965. *Snoopy Come Home*, 1963. Soft cover. Books by Charles Schulz. Holt/Rinehart and Winston. $18-20 each.

Peanuts Every Sunday book by Holt, Rinehart and Winston, Inc. 9th printing. First published April, 1961. Around 1960 Rinehart & Co; Inc. became Holt, Rinehart & Winston Inc. Naturally early editions are most valued. $8-12.

Book. Special Anniversary Edition. *Love is Walking Hand in Hand*. First published by Determined in 1965. This edition was published by Ballantine Books, a division of Random House. This first Topper Books edition was published in 1987 and designed by Determined. $10-12 paperback.

Good Grief, More Peanuts! book. Holt, Rinehart and Winston. $8-12.
1st published-August 1957. Holt, Rinehart & Co. Inc. 22nd printing.
1967.

Christmas is Together Time story book. 1964. Determined. $15-20.

Peanuts Cook Book. Determined. 1969. $15-20.

Charlie Brown's All-Stars
storybook. World publishing co.
1966. $15-25 Depending on edition
and condition.

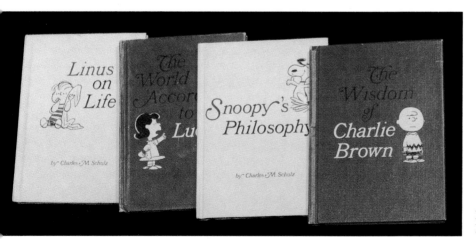

Peanut Philosophers books.
Hallmark. 1972. $20-25 set.

Charlie Brown Philosophy books.
Hallmark. 1972. $20-25 set.

Peanut Philosophers set
of books. Hallmark.
1972. $20-25 set.

Happy Birthday, Charlie Brown: 30 Years in Comic Strip, 15 Years on Television. Lee Mendelson with Charles Schulz Random House. 1979. $30-40.

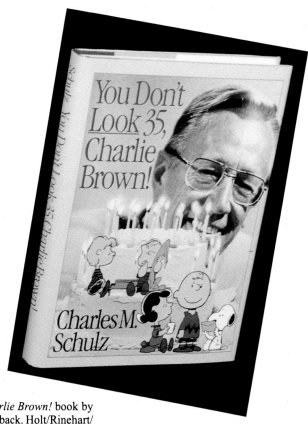

You don't look 35, Charlie Brown! book by
Charles Schulz. Hardback. Holt/Rinehart/
and Winston. 1985. $30-40.

PEANUTS JUBILEE
My Life and Art
with Charlie Brown and Others
By Charles M. Schulz

Peanuts Jubilee, My Life and Art with Charlie Brown and Others by Charles Schulz. 1975. Hardback 11-1/2" x 16". Holt/Rinehart and Winston. $75-100.

But We Love You, Charlie Brown

a *PEANUTS* book by Charles M. Schulz

But We Love You, Charlie Brown. Fortunately for our children and young adults, Weekly Reader Books, presented many Peanuts Books. Bound in hard cover for durability, and the volume of copies made these easy to process. First published in 1959. Late 1970s early 1980s. $3-9 each.

HE PEANUTS TRIVIA
REFERENCE BOOK
Monte Schulz & Jody Millward

n introduced Schroeder to the piano? • *Which character drew his own comic strip?*
o invented the "schmuckle ball"? • *Why was Snoopy reported to the Head Beagle?*

EXPERT PANEL
(ASK US ANYTHING)

The Peanuts Trivia & Reference Book. Monte Schulz & Jody Millward. Henry Holt and Co. Paperback. 1986. $10-15.

The Parables of Peanuts by Robert L. Short. Harper and Roe Publishers. Over 250 cartoons making theology enjoyable. 1968. $20-30.

Thompson Is in Trouble, Charlie Brown

a *PEANUTS* book by Charles M. Schulz

Thompson Is in Trouble, Charlie Brown story book. For Weekly Reader Books. Holt/Rinehart and Winston. 1972. $3-9.

$1.95

The Parables of
Peanuts.

Robert L. Short

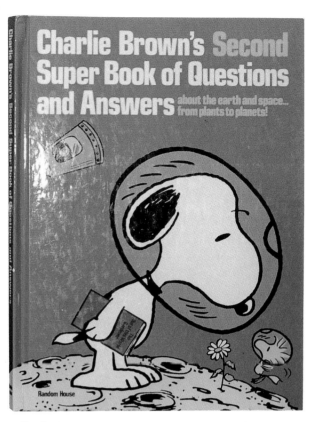

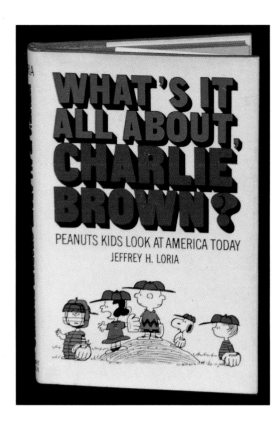

What's It All About, Charlie Brown?. 1st edition. 1968. $20-25.

Charlie Brown's Second Super Book of Questions and Answers. Random House. Hardbound. 1977. $10-15.

Cardboard flip books, on a metal ring. Hallmark. Early 1970s. $10-15.

Christmas Time with Snoopy and His Friends, pop up story book. Hallmark. Mid 1980s. $25-35.

Pet Belle book. Determined. Mid 1980s. Also available *Pet Snoopy.* $10-15.

A Charlie Brown Christmas storybook. Fortunately for school children Scholastic made these comic book sized booklets featuring nearly all of the Charlie Brown specials. 1970s/80s. $3-5.

Golden book, *A Charlie Brown Christmas*. Hardbound. 1988. $7-10.

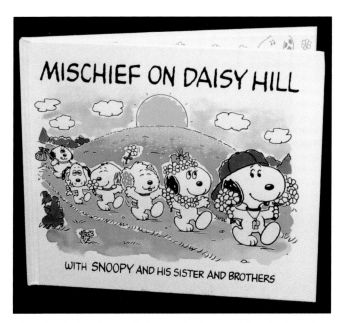

Storybook, *Mischief on Daisy Hill*, hardcover. Determined. 1993. $15-20.

Christmas Is Together Time paperback book by Charles Schulz. 1983. Determined. $10-12.

Snoopy mini story books. 1993. American Education Publishing. $4-6.

Peanut gang book set.
Harper Collins. 1996.
$4-5 each.

The following six photographs: Videos. In the early 1980s videos gained much popularity. Peanuts videos were released and released by various companies throughout this time. Hi-Tops video, Paramount, KVC-Kartes Video Communications. Many were digitally remastered for excellent sound and picture quality. Mint in cello wrap is best but most collectors like to view these wonderful features. 1980s early 1990s. $15-20 each.

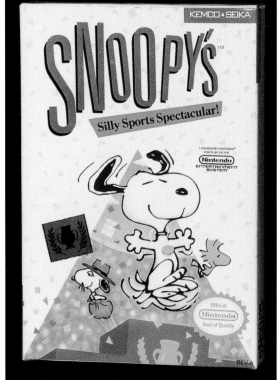

"Snoopy's Silly Sports Spectacular!"
Nintendo game. Early 1980s. In order
to play you must use an original
Nintendo system. $60-80.

Showtime, Woodstock

Program to Broadway play. 1970s. $12-15.

Stage play program from
Fox Little Theater, in San
Francisco. 1972. $10-15.

Lobby cards. "Snoopy Come Home" for Paramount. 1972. $9-12 each or $70-
90 for the full set of eight. This was the second motion picture made.

Movie lobby cards from "Snoopy Come Home". Paramount. 1972. $9-12 each or $70-90 for the full set of eight.

Movie souvenir, "A Boy Named Charlie Brown". 1969. $10-15.

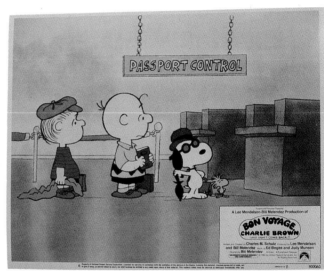

Above four photographs: Movie lobby cards from "Bon Voyage, Charlie Brown". Paramount. 1980. $9-12 each or $70-90 for the full set of eight. This was the fourth motion picture made.

"Bon Voyage, Charlie Brown," show cards. Fourth Peanuts feature
motion picture. Paramount. 1980. $9-12 each. $70-90 full set.

The following eight photographs: Movie lobby cards from "A Boy Named Charlie Brown". Paramount. 1969. $9-12 each or $70-90 for the set of eight. This was the first Peanuts movie.

Charlie Brown
and the
'Peanuts' Gang
in their
First Movie!

"A Boy Named Charlie Brown"

Charlie Brown
and the
'Peanuts' Gang
in their
First Movie!

"A Boy Named Charlie Brown"

Charlie Brown
and the
'Peanuts' Gang
in their
First Movie!

"A Boy Named Charlie Brown"

Charlie Brown
and the
'Peanuts' Gang
in their
First Movie!

"A Boy Named Charlie Brown"

The following eight photographs: Movie posters. "Race for Your Life, Charlie Brown." Third Peanuts feature motion picture for Paramount. 1977. $9-12 each. $70-90 full set of eight.

Bibliography

Johnson, Rheta Grinslay. *Good Grief: The Story of Charles Schulz.* New York: Pharos Books, 1989. Pharos Book. New York.

Fanning, Jim. *Boomer Magazine*, April, 1995. Dubuque, Iowa: Antique Trader Publicatons. Dubuque, Iowa.

Holt, Charles M. *You Don't Look 35 Charlie Brown.* New York: Holt, Rinehart, Winston, 1985.

Wooden Lucy coat rack. Probably Determined. 1970s. $15-20.